CONTEMPORARY'S

EDGE ON ENGLISH

ALL
SPELLED
OUT

D

Betsy Rubin

Project Editor
Deborah M. Newton Chocolate

Published by Contemporary Books, Inc.
Two Prudential Plaza, Chicago, Illinois 60601-6790
Manufactured in the United States of America
International Standard Book Number: 0-8092-4964-2

Published simultaneously in Canada by
Fitzhenry & Whiteside
195 Allstate Parkway
Markham, Ontario L3R 4T8
Canada

Editorial Director
Caren Van Slyke

Editorial
Julie Landau
Christine M. Benton

Production Editor
J. D. Fairbanks

Art & Production
Princess Louise El
Lois Koehler

Cover Design
William Ewing

Contents

TO THE INSTRUCTOR _v_
TO THE STUDENT _vii_
DIAGNOSTIC TEST _ix_
    Introduction to Spelling Skills _2_

SECTION 1
    Special Consonant Sounds 1: "S" Sound   _5_
    Special Consonant Sounds 2: "Z" Sound   _8_
    Special Consonant Sounds 3: "SH" Sound   _11_
    Special Consonant Sounds 4: "CH" Sound   _14_
    Special Consonant Sounds 5: "ZH" Sound   _15_
    Special Consonant Sounds 6: "J" Sound   _17_
    Special Consonant Sounds 7: "F" Sound   _19_
    Special Consonant Sounds 8: "K" Sound   _21_
    Looking Up Spellings _23_
    Double Consonants _25_
    Silent Consonants _32_
    Review of Consonants _36_
    A Letter of Thanks _37_

SECTION 2
    Silent Vowels _38_
    Letter to a School _41_
    Spelling That Doesn't Match the Pronunciation _42_
    Spelling Errors Related to Pronunciation _47_
    Review of Silent Vowels and Pronunciation Spelling Errors _55_
    Reduced Vowel Roots 1: A   _56_
    Reduced Vowel Roots 2: E   _58_
    Reduced Vowel Roots 3: ER   _60_
    Reduced Vowel Roots 4: I   _61_
    Reduced Vowel Roots 5: O   _63_
    Reduced Vowel Roots 6: OR   _64_
    Reduced Vowel Roots 7: U   _65_
    Reduced Vowel Suffixes 1: ENT/ENCE and ANT/ANCE   _67_
    Reduced Vowel Suffixes 2: OR and AR   _70_
    Reduced Vowel Suffixes 3: ABLE/IBLE   _73_
    Reduced Vowel Suffixes 4: LE/EL/AL   _75_
    Reduced Vowel Suffixes 5: ARY/ERY/ORY   _78_
    Reduced Vowel Suffixes 6: AIN/ON/OM   _80_
    Reduced Vowel Suffixes 7: ACY/ASY   _81_
    Reduced Vowel Suffixes 8: Tricky Endings   _82_
    Getting Lost in Long Words _84_
    Past Tense and Past Participles _85_
    Finding Difficult Past Forms and Past Participles _90_
    Review Test _91_

SECTION 3

Words that Sound Alike **92**

Contractions and Possessives **100**

Words that Sound Almost Alike **104**

A Letter of Complaint **109**

Words that Look Almost Alike **110**

Finding Confusing Words **116**

Words with ALL and AL **117**

Dealing with Hard-to-Spell Names **119**

Review Test **120**

FINAL TEST **121**

ANSWER KEY **123**

500 COMMONLY MISSPELLED WORDS **130**

To the Instructor

How well we spell affects the overall impact of our writing. For this reason, spelling is a necessary component of any writing program. Nevertheless, this component has sometimes been neglected because the English spelling system can seem too overwhelming to teach. Although our spelling system is indeed complex, adult and teenage students *can* learn to become better spellers.

A realistic approach to teaching spelling begins with instruction in useful rules and guidelines that allow students to spell hundreds of words. These will not help in every situation, however. Since our language is derived from many sources, the spelling of different words may be governed by esoteric rules that apply to limited numbers of words. In such cases, it is best to concentrate on teaching the spellings of the words themselves. Finally, all good spellers make use of the dictionary when they are uncertain about a particular spelling. This book, then, includes the following types of instruction:

1) Rules and guidelines that are highly productive in many cases
2) Specific words that are commonly misspelled and that do not follow clear-cut rules
3) Dictionary skills

All Spelled Out—C and *D* are based on a list of 500 commonly misspelled words. The commonly misspelled words are indicated as "Words to Know" in the beginning of a lesson. These words have an asterisk (*) next to them when they appear in the text. To be chosen for the list, words had to be not only commonly misspelled, but also commonly used. (Thus, a word like *student* would not appear because it is not frequently misspelled, and a word like *globulin* would not appear because it is not frequently used.)

Students practice all of these words as they work through the exercises in the book. Although students are expected to know all of the words by the end of the book, instruction is not limited to the word list. Students also practice applying rules to produce words not found on the list.

Scope

This book, written with teens and adults in mind, assumes a knowledge of some basic spelling rules and patterns. Students should already be familiar with rules governing the spelling of one-syllable words. (If they aren't, you will probably wish to begin with *All Spelled Out—A* and *B*.)

The introduction acquaints the student with basic spelling skills. Section 1 is concerned with special consonant sounds, double consonants, and silent consonants. Section 2 presents some commonly misspelled words with reduced vowels in the suffix and words with reduced vowels in the roots. These words pose problems for students because the reduced vowel sound can be represented by any reduced vowel letter. Since students will need to learn which words use which letters for the reduced vowel sound, the words are grouped together by vowel letters for ease of learning. Also presented in Section 2 are silent vowels, words with spellings that don't match the pronunciation, spelling errors related to pronunciation, and past forms and past participles. Finally, Section 3 focuses on words that sound alike, on words that sound *almost* alike, and on words that *look* almost alike.

Interspersed throughout the book are dictionary skills exercises that teach students how to find the spellings of words and their derivations. In addition, there are special exercises, called "Words for Now," that focus on words useful in everyday writing tasks such as filling out applications and composing formal letters. The appendix contains a list of 500 commonly misspelled words.

Organization

Most lessons begin with an introduction, in which students focus on the spelling issue that will be covered. If there is a rule, students learn and practice it. The next step is the "Say-Copy-Check" exercise, in which students copy each word, concentrating on the hard parts.

Finally, students complete freer exercises, including fill-in-the-blanks, sentence writing, proofreading, and word games. Mnemonic devices (called "spelling tricks") are provided to help students recall especially difficult spellings. Students also have a chance to write their own spelling tricks.

How To Use This Book

This book can be used by individuals working at their own pace or by the class as a whole. If you take the first approach, you should direct individual students to the chapters they need to concentrate on according to the results they obtain on the diagnostic test. If the class is working through the book together, the diagnostic test will indicate which areas the group needs to work on. (In either case, it is advisable to complete all sections of the book, spending more time on difficult areas and less on easier areas.) When working with the entire class, go through the introductory material together. Students should then do the exercises individually.

In addition to the tests provided in the book, you should give dictation quizzes especially focusing on word list words. Choose ten to twenty words per quiz. Read each word out loud clearly. Then give the word in the context of a sentence, so that students are sure of what word they are being asked to write. Lastly, repeat the word. For example: "Council. The city council met on Friday. Council." A more difficult dictation quiz would require students to write an entire sentence. Just make sure that all hard words have been studied in advance.

It is not necessary to restrict the class to the word list. If there are other words you feel your students should know, teach these words and include them on your quizzes. Encourage students to make up their own lists of spellings they wish to learn.

As noted before, spelling is not an end in itself but is rather an important part of writing well. For this reason, a spelling program should be connected to a writing program. Students should be expected to use correct spelling in their compositions and other writing projects.

Related Skills

Spelling is intimately connected to three other areas: grammar, vocabulary, and pronunciation. Regarding grammar, make sure that students understand how to use parts of speech and the different tenses. It would be useless, for example, to teach the spelling of a word like *occasionally* if a student cannot use the word in a sentence. Similarly, students must know how to use past forms if the spelling of **ed** endings on verbs is to be useful.

Students must already be familiar with the meaning of a word before they can learn to spell it. Therefore, if you note any vocabulary problems, give the students extra instruction so that they are familiar with each word before they are required to learn its spelling.

The issue of pronunciation and spelling can be sticky. In this large country, there are often different acceptable ways to pronounce a word. Do not attempt, therefore, to "correct" a student's pronunciation or imply that a student "speaks badly." You may, however, ask students to imitate a certain pronunciation for the *purposes of learning a spelling*. For example, in actual speech, most people reduce the first e of the word *interest*, so that it sounds like "intrest." This pronunciation is both common and acceptable (see your dictionary!). For the purpose of learning the spelling, you can ask students to "overpronounce" the word in isolation. That is, ask them to say each syllable slowly and deliberately as follows: "in-ter-est." This oral exercise will help them to remember to write that reduced e.

Finally, encourage independence. Have students take responsibility for their own spelling by keeping personal lists of spellings they wish to learn. Students should keep a spelling notebook for these lists and for exercises from the textbook. Insist that students buy a pocket dictionary, carry it at all times, and use it! The dictionary may be the most valuable tool for spelling independence.

In helping students work through this book, it is important to stress the goal of spelling improvement. No one becomes a perfect speller (that's one reason we have dictionaries!), but anyone can become a better speller.

Spelling and Your Image

Most of us are concerned about the image we project. We choose our clothes carefully and try to behave in a way that inspires respect. Appearance and behavior are not the only standards by which we are judged. Our writing, too, is important.

Imagine that you are applying for a job or for admission to a school. If your application is written messily and is full of poor grammar and spelling errors, what impression will the reader have? Will your application be accepted? Probably not. On the other hand, a neatly typed application with correct grammar and spelling will put you in the running.

Good spelling is an important part of your image. It makes you look competent and responsible.

Anyone Can Be a Better Speller

"But I've always been a terrible speller."
"Our spelling system has no rules."
"It's hopeless—I'll never learn to spell!"

It's true that the English spelling system is complex, but the fact is, *anyone can become a better speller*—yes, even you! You may not realize it, but you already know lots and lots of spelling rules subconsciously. For example, does this word look right?

aktiv

No! Your mind knows that *k* does not usually appear in the middle of the word and that *v* does not occur at the end of a word. The correct spelling is, of course, *active*—with the letter *c* in the middle of the word and the letter *e* after *v*. There are many other rules like this that you use in spelling without even realizing it.

Sometimes your subconscious mind doesn't have all the answers, though. Things can get a little trickier in some situations. For instance, which is correct:

aggresive? agressive? aggressive?

dilema? dilemma? dillemma?

The *All Spelled Out* series will help you deal with difficult spellings like these. You will learn general guidelines and rules that govern spellings like *aggressive*. When the rules are obscure, as they are for the word *dilemma*, you will learn the problem word itself—and it won't be as hard as you think!

The Set-Up

The introduction of this book presents you with spelling and dictionary skills. Section 1 focuses on the many different ways to spell consonant sounds and on problems with double consonants and silent consonants. If you're often confused about which letter to use to spell a sound, Section 2 will introduce you to silent vowels, reduced vowel roots, and reduced vowel suffixes. You will also learn how to make the past forms of verbs. Finally, Section 3 will show you how to choose the correct spelling when two words look or sound alike.

At the end of the book, you'll find a list of 500 frequently misspelled words. Each of these 500 words is taught in either *All Spelled Out— C* or its companion volume, *All Spelled Out— D*. If you work through all the lessons carefully, you should be able to spell every word on the list. Words from this list will be marked with an asterisk (*) when they appear in the text. The asterisk is your signal to pay particular attention to a word. In addition, there are sets of often confused words which you'll also know by the time you finish *All Spelled Out— D*.

The Keys to Spelling

Improving your spelling is a matter of improving your understanding of the spelling system. It's also a matter of improving your observation skills. *All Spelled Out* will show you how to sharpen both your understanding and your skills.

Now, can you ever reach *absolute perfection* in spelling? Probably not—few, if any, people do. At times, everyone has a question about the proper spelling of a word. What's the most reliable way to find out? Use the dictionary! *All Spelled Out* will teach you how to use the dictionary quickly and effectively to improve your spelling.

Finally, this book presents special exercises (called Words for Now) that teach groups of words that are essential for completing school and job applications and writing formal letters. These exercises help you to learn the special words that, when spelled correctly, will help you project a strong image.

In summary, *All Spelled Out* covers five areas.

1. General spelling rules and guidelines
2. Specific problem words
3. Dictionary skills
4. Words to Use (special words for everyday writing tasks)
5. Words for Now (special words for letters and applications)

Developing Your Own Spelling Program

No spelling book can give you *every* word you need to know. Each person has his or her own "spelling monsters."

Buy a notebook to fill up and keep. Use the notebook not only to write words and sentences from this textbook, but also to keep a list of any other words you need to know.

This way you can personalize your spelling program. Keep in mind that the skills you'll develop by working through *All Spelled Out* will help you attack your personal spelling monsters.

And now—are you ready for success? If so, turn to the Diagnostic Test. Good luck!

Diagnostic Test

PART I—25 points
Read the sentence and write the complete missing word. The letters in parentheses give you a clue. You must supply one or more missing letters.

1. The patient's resistance has lowered; making him more _____ to infection. (su—eptible)

2. You'll need to _____ the position that is available with your firm. (advert—e)

3. Crafting stained glass that way is a difficult _____. (tec—ni—ue)

4. Phuoc Pham was in a _____ over what to do about losing his passport. (dile—a)

5. Don't _____ them by begging for money. (emba—ass)

6. She has a painting on _____ in the art show. (ex—bit)

7. He tried to demonstrate his affection for her in very _____ ways. (s—tle)

8. When we first bought our home we didn't have a high _____ payment. (mor—age)

9. I was so tired I fell like a brick into my bed from _____. (fati—)

10. My baby brother is a pest and a _____. (n—sance)

11. Her wedding gown was white; this was her first _____. (marr—ge)

12. The _____ shouted army orders to the new recruits. (s—rg—nt)

13. The referee asked the two boxers to retire to _____ corners. (n—tral)

14. The tank of his car was empty; he needed some _____. (gas–line)

15. The home _____ is important when it comes to raising children. (Envi—ment)

16. His birthday is on the _____ of March. (twe—h)

17. "When up on the housetop what should appear, but a _____ sleigh and eight tiny reindeer." (min—ture)

18. *Sports Illlustrated* is the title of a _____. (mag—zine)

19. I prefer the summer months when the _____ is higher. (temp—ture)

20. There was a terrible _____ on the expressway this morning. (acc—dent)

21. _____ is my favorite day of the week. (Sat—rday)

22. My roommate wakes me up at odd hours of the night. He is very rude and _____ of good manners. (ignor—t)

23. Some people feel that former President Nixon was largely _____ for the Watergate break-in. (respons—ble)

24. Always use a _____ letter at the beginning of a sentence. (capit—l)

25. Dr. Martin Luther King and Mahatma Ghandi fought racism and _____ in the U.S. and India. (prejud—)

PART II—10 points
Complete each sentence with the correct *irregular* past form of the word in parentheses.

Example: My husband *built* the boys a tree house. (build)

26. He _____ his Korean friend a long letter yesterday. (write)

27. The defense attorney _____ that the newspapers convicted his client. (say)

28. She _____ him that she loved him. (tell)

29. We _____ our teacher a big red apple. (buy)

30. The "Refrigerator" _____ a pass and scored a touchdown. (catch)

31. Flannery O 'Connor and William Faulkner _____ Southern writers. (be)

32. His laughter _____ the walls like thunder. (shake)

33. The War of 1812 was _____ between the U.S. and England. (fight)

34. The students _____ that a verb was a place. (think)

35. We _____ the porch because it was covered with leaves. (sweep)

PART III—5 points
Write the missing past participle of the word in parentheses.

36. April had already _____ her homework. (do)

37. She had _____ the book home from school. (take)

38. We've _____ checks for too much money this month. (write)

39. He has _____ very ill this past winter. (be)

40. She has _____ me for a long time. (know)

PART IV—10 points
Fill in the correct word in the sentences below. Use one of the words in the parentheses.

41. The groom and bride walked to the _____.
    (alter, altar)

42. The girl paid the boy a nice _____.
    (complement, compliment)

43. The _____ in the theater was so narrow it was difficult to pass through.
    (isle, aisle)

44. I wrote him a long letter. I asked him to _____ my apology.
    (accept, except)

45. I have a _____ of my great-grandfather's cousin, Marietta Wilkerson.
    (pitcher, picture)

46. Love has a very powerful _____ upon people.
    (affect, effect)

47. Please put the _____ in the hamper.
    (close, clothes)

48. "Mom, what are we having for _____?"
    (dessert, desert)

49. We'll need to carefully think _____ these considerations next time.
    (thorough, through)

50. Always use a _____ to separate items in a series.
    (coma, comma)

Answers start on page 123.

Diagnostic Test Chart

The chart below shows the number of each question on the test and the section in which the material is covered.

Circle the number of each question you missed. If you miss more than two spellings in a section, you will need to pay special attention to that section in the text.

ITEMS					SECTION TO STUDY	
1	2	3			Section 1:	Special Consonant Sounds
4	5				Section 1:	Double Consonants
6	7	8			Section 1:	Silent Consonants
9	10	11			Section 2:	Silent Vowels
12	13	14			Section 2:	Spelling That Doesn't Match Pronunciation
15	16	17			Section 2:	Spelling Errors Related to Pronunciation
18	19	20	21		Section 2:	Reduced Vowel Roots
22	23	24	25		Section 2:	Reduced Vowel Suffixes
26 31	27 32	28 33	29 34	30 35	Section 2:	Past Forms
36	37	38	39	40	Section 2:	Past Participles
41	42	43			Section 3:	Words that Sound Alike
44	45	46			Section 3:	Words that Sound Almost Alike
47	48	49	50		Section 3:	Words that Look Almost Alike

CONTEMPORARY'S

EDGE ON ENGLISH

ALL
SPELLED
OUT

D

Introduction to Spelling Skills

Say-Copy-Check

To be a good speller, you must do two things: learn to spell new words and **remember** how to spell them. How do you **learn** the spelling of a word? Close observation is the key.

Let's say you want to learn these spellings:

annual   enemy   prefer

You can use a simple procedure called the **Say-Copy-Check** exercise. First, look at each word carefully, noticing its shape and length. Study the different shape and length of the word *annual* as compared to another word. Boxes have been used to bring out the differences:

a|n|n|u|a|l   v|a|l|l|e|y

As you study the word, say it out loud so that you can pair the sight and the sound of the word in your mind. Knowing how to pronounce a word correctly can actually make you a better speller.

Next, copy the word carefully in your spelling notebook. (For practice now, however, you'll write the words right on this page instead of in your notebook.) If certain parts of the word seem hard to you, write those parts in **capital letters.** Then copy the word again in small letters.

Here is an example: annual ___*aNNual*___   ___*annual*___

Copy the example here: _____ _____ Now check back, letter by letter, to make sure you have written the word correctly.

Try the Say-Copy-Check exercise with the next word. Use the spaces provided below to copy the word twice. In the first space, copy the words using capital letters for the hard part in bold type. Then copy the word again in small letters.

    enemy _____ _____

Do one more example:

    prefer _____ _____

Spelling Tricks

You have studied the spelling of three new words, but how will you remember them? One way to keep a hard word in your mind is to make up a spelling trick. For example, in order to remember that *annual* has two *n*s, you might think of the following sentence:

ANN has an *aNNual* party.

This helps you to remember the sound of the *n*s in *annual*.
To remember the *e* in *enemy,* you could think of this sentence:

FrEE the *EnEmy*.

This book will give you many such spelling tricks to write in your notebook and remember, but you'll also want to invent and write down your own. Try it now. Can you think of a spelling trick to remind yourself that *prefer* starts with *pre*? (Hint: Use the word *pretzel.*) Write your spelling trick on the line.

_____

_____

Will you need to make up a spelling trick for every word you want to learn? No. You can learn many words without this extra step. Also, it's easier to think up spelling tricks for some words than for others. So just use spelling tricks when you are able to or when you need to.

Which Looks Right?

Days after learning a new word, you might need to write it. How will you remember the spelling? Think back to the time you copied it into your notebook. Try to recall what it looked like on the page. Remember the spelling trick, if there was one. Then, if you are still not sure, write down the different ways you think the word might be spelled. For example:

anual   *annual*   *ennual*

Which one looks right? You probably saw right away that the second word has the correct spelling because very often your eyes will recognize the right spelling. See if your eyes can recognize the correct spellings of the two other words you've just studied. Circle the correct spellings.

enamy   *enumy*   *enemy*   *prefer*   *perfer*   *pefer*

━━━━━━━━━━━━━━━━ PRACTICE 1 ━━━━━━━━━━━━━━━━

Now learn the following four words. Using your notebook this time, do the Say-Copy-Check exercise. Use capital letters for the hard parts and try to think of some spelling tricks to help you. Use the hints if you'd like.

against _____
(Hint: Use *gain* in your spelling trick.)

tenant _____
(Hint: Use *ten* in your spelling trick.)

acknowledge _____
(Hint: Use *know* in your spelling trick.)

standard _____
(Hint: Use *card* in your spelling trick.)

Once you have finished this exercise, look at these alternatives and let your eyes recognize the correct spelling. Circle the right spellings.

a. *against*   *aganst*   *agianst*

b. *tinant*   *tienant*   *tenant*

c. *aknoledge*   *akcnowledge*   *acknowledge*

d. *standerd*   *standard*   *standird*

Proofread

When you know how to spell a word, does this mean you will always spell it correctly? Not necessarily. It's easy to make a spelling mistake even on a simple word if you are writing quickly or if you aren't paying attention. Therefore, a very important spelling skill is **proofreading.** Always go back and read over what you have written. Be especially careful with long words or words you've had trouble with before.

PRACTICE 2

Proofread the following paragraph. If you see a word spelled wrong, cross it out and write the correct word above it. There are five errors. The first one has been corrected for you.

tenant
My brother is a ~~tinant~~ in a lovely North Shore apartment building. His anual lease will expire in February. He signed a standerd lease that acknoledges no increase in the rate of his rent. He will probably renew his lease since he perfers to maintain a reasonable rent rate.

Use The Dictionary

There's another important spelling skill: using the dictionary. The dictionary will show you how to spell new words, and it will also help you check the spelling of words you've already studied. This book provides several excercises to sharpen your dictionary skills.

REMEMBER THE FIVE SPELLING SKILLS:

1. USE THE SAY-COPY-CHECK EXERCISE.

2. USE SPELLING TRICKS.

3. SEE WHICH SPELLING LOOKS RIGHT.

4. PROOFREAD.

5. USE THE DICTIONARY.

Answers start on page 123.

Word Parts   Sounds to Spell

Special Consonant Sounds   *Double Consonants*

Dictionary Exercise   *Silent Consonants*

Looking Up Spellings   Words for Now

                A Letter of Thanks

SOUNDS TO SPELL

Special Consonant Sounds 1: "S" Sound

As we noted in the introduction, one sound can sometimes be spelled in several ways. In this section, we'll go through eight sounds with multiple spellings.

WORDS TO KNOW

*absence	*discipline	*muscle	*since
*ancestor	*fascinate	*necessary	*society
*circle	*grocery	*scene	*source
*citizen	*license	*science	*susceptible
*city	*medicine	*scissors	

Sam's absence from **science class** was **noticeable.**

Read the sentence above out loud and notice the "S" sounds in the words in bold type. The "S" sound can be made with these letters or combinations:

S SS SC C

Look carefully at the *c* and *sc* spellings in the sentence. They sound like "S" only before the letter *e* (*absenCE, notiCEable*) or the letter *i* (*SCIence*).

Guide: To make the "S" sound, we use *s* or *ss*. We can also use *c* or *sc* plus *e/i*.

5

Circle the letters *s*, *ss*, and *c* in these words. Then do the Say-Copy-Check exercise, capitalizing these letters the first time you copy the word.

*absence _abSenCe_   _absence_   *license _____

*ancestor _____   *medicine _____

*circle _____   *necessary _____

*citizen _____   *society _____

*city _____   *source _____

*grocery _____

Here are some spelling tricks. To remember the c in medicine, think of this phrase:

medICal medICine

Fill in the missing letters and then copy the trick into your notebook.

med____al med____ine

To remember the *cess* in *necessary*, we'll make up a woman's name, Cessa:

CESSA says it's neCESSAry.

Fill in the missing letters and then copy the trick into your notebook:

_____ says it's ne_____ry.

━━━━━━━━━━━━━━ PRACTICE 1 ━━━━━━━━━━━━━━

Fill in the missing words with the "S" sound that you've just studied.

a. Are you a _____*citizen*_____ of the United States?

b. She got her driver's_____.

c. Take this _____ every day, and you'll feel better.

d. Los Angeles is a big_____.

e. One of my_____s was a pioneer.

f. He got kicked out of school because of all of his_____s.

g. You don't need to explain. It's not _____.

h. Let's try to find the _____ of this problem.

i. We have to go to the _____ store.

j. Do you think that _____ is to blame for the high crime rate?

k. She drew a _____ and a square.

Now study the *sc* words. Circle the *sc* and do the Say-Copy-Check exercise, capitalizing *sc* the first time.

*discipline _____

*fascinate _____

*muscle _____

*scene _____

*scissors _____

*susceptible _____

Note that *muscle* is an exception word. It does not have *e* or *i* after the *sc*. To remember the *sc* in *muscle,* think of the word *muscular:*

a *muSCular muSCle*

Fill in the missing letters of the spelling trick and then copy it in your notebook:

a mu____ular mu____le

━━━━━━━━━━━━━━━━━ PRACTICE 2 ━━━━━━━━━━━━━━
Fill in the missing *sc* words you have studied.

a. He is _____ to many diseases.

b. She cut her hair with a pair of old _____.

c. Don't make a _____ in front of all these people!

d. You _____ me, darling.

e. It takes a lot of _____ to lift a piano!

f. Do you believe in strict _____ for children?

Watch out for two words that are sometimes confused: *since* and *science*. They are pronounced and spelled differently and have different meanings: *since* refers to time, as in "since Monday." *Science* is a subject or field, like biology or chemistry. Write a sentence with each word:

_____

_____

Answers start on page 123.

7

Special Consonant Sounds 2: "Z" Sound

<table>
<tr><td rowspan="5">WORDS
TO
KNOW</td><td>*advertise</td><td>*exercise</td><td>*recognize</td></tr>
<tr><td>*analyze</td><td>*pleasant</td><td>*surprise</td></tr>
<tr><td>*apologize</td><td>*possession</td><td>*visible</td></tr>
<tr><td>*criticism</td><td>*presence</td><td>*wisdom</td></tr>
<tr><td>*criticize</td><td></td><td></td></tr>
</table>

A **zebra** was **visible** on the African plain.

Read the sentence above and listen to the "Z" sound in the two words in bold type. It's not surprising that z is used to spell the "Z" sound (*Zebra*), but note that s is also used for this sound (*viSible*).

> **Guide:** Both s and z are used to spell the "Z" sound, but s is used more often than z.

Circle the s that has the "Z" sound. Do the Say-Copy-Check exercise, capitalizing the s the first time.

*criticism _____

*pleasant _____

*presence _____

*visible _____

*wisdom _____

Now write a spelling trick to help you remember the s in *pleasant*. (Hint: Use the word *please*.)

_____

Copy this trick into your notebook.

   Watch out for the spellings of *possession* and *scissors*. The double s in *scissors* and the first double s in *possession* sound like "Z." Circle the first ss and do the Say-Copy-Check exercise:

*possession _____

*scissors _____

Fill in the missing "Z" sound words that you have studied.

a. Your very _____ is comforting.

b. The weather was sunny and _____.

c. Great _____ can come with old age.

d. She can't take any _____—even if it's constructive.

e. Put reflectors on your bike so it will be _____ at night.

f. Cut the ribbon with the _____.

g. The bank took _____ of the house.

ISE, IZE, YZE Endings

Advertise your product, but don't **criticize** the other brand.

Note the two endings in the bold-type words; *ise* and *ize* are pronounced alike. *Ize* is more common, but many words are spelled with *ise*. There is no rule to tell you when to use one or the other, but if you study these words, you'll have mastered the most troublesome ones.
    Circle *ize* or *ise* and do the Say-Copy-Check exercise.

*apologize _____

*criticize _____

*recognize _____

*advertise _____

*exercise _____

*surprise _____

There is one word with *yze:*

*analyze _____

Fill in the missing words that end in *ise*, *ize* or *yze*.

a. Both _____ and a low-fat diet will help you lose weight.

b. I almost didn't _____ you with your new haircut!

c. All he does is _____. He never says anything positive.

d. I want to _____ for my bad behavior.

e. They gave me a _____ party.

f. Should doctors and lawyers _____ their services on TV?

g. Let's _____ the problem.

PROOFREAD

Keeping in mind all of the "Z" sound words you've learned, read each sentence below. If it is correct, write *OK*. If a word is misspelled, cross out the word and rewrite it on the line.

a. Her ~~wizdom~~ was great. _____ *wisdom* _____

b. She acts as if her husband were her possession. _____ *OK* _____

c. What a wonderful surprize! _____

d. We had a pleasant conversation. _____

e. I hate to exercize. _____

f. We watched the plane until it was no longer vizible. _____

g. I refuse to apolgyze for *your* mistake. _____

h. Don't criticize her so much. _____

i. Constructive criticizm can be helpful. _____

j. We need to analize the results. _____

k. Many companies advertize their products on TV. _____

l. I feel a ghostly presence in this room. _____

Answers start on page 123.

Special Consonant Sounds 3: "SH" Sound

WORDS TO KNOW	*admission	*education	*machine	*physician
	*associate	*efficient	*ocean	*precious
	*corporation	*financial	*official	*prediction
	*delicious	*insurance	*permission	*sufficient

She is such an **efficient insurance** agent that her **corporation** gave her **permission** to open her own branch office.

Read the sentence out loud and notice how the "SH" sound is spelled in the bold-type words. These words show most of the ways that "SH" can be spelled.

> **Guide:** In short words (*she, wash*), the "SH" sound is spelled with the letters *sh*. In longer words (*permission, corporation, efficient, insurance*), other letter combinations are used to spell this sound.

TI Combination

Tion is a common word ending that sounds like "shun." Circle the *tion* ending in these words and do the Say-Copy-Check exercise:

*corporation _____

*education _____

*prediction _____

Tial sounds like "shull." Circle *tial* and do the Say-Copy-Check exercise:

partial _____ spatial _____

SSI Combination

Ssion is another way to spell the "shun" sound. It appears in the word *mission*. Circle *ssion* and do the Say-Copy-Check exercise:

*admission _____ passion _____

mission _____ *permission _____

11

Fill in the correct *ti* or *ssi* word that you've studied.

a. The astrologer's _____ did not come true.

b. A good _____ will help you get a good job.

c. I got special _____ to leave early.

d. The _____ has two thousand employees.

e. The _____ fee is $5.

f. This is only a _____ report. It's not complete.

CI Combination

Ci sounds like "SH" in the combinations *cial, cian, cien,* and *cious.* Circle the *ci* in each word and do the Say-Copy-Check exercise.

*efficient _____   *physician _____

*financial _____   *precious _____

musician _____   special _____

*official _____   *sufficient _____

The word *associate* has two possible pronunciations. The *c* can sound like "SH" or like "S." Either way, learn how to spell it right.

*associate _____

Read the definition and fill in the correct *ci* word.

a. singer or instrument player: _____

b. related to money: _____

c. enough: _____

d. very valuable: _____

e. doctor: _____

f. formal: _____

g. unique: _____

SU Combination

In some words, *su* spells the "SH" sound. Circle *su* and do the Say-Copy-Check exercise:

sure _____

*insurance _____

pressure _____

Other Spellings

There are still other spellings for the "SH" sound. Circle the underlined letters in these words and do the Say-Copy-Check exercise. Capitalize the underlined letters the first time you copy the word.

*machine _____   *ocean _____

PRACTICE 3

Fill in the missing "SH" sound word with the *su* and other spellings.

a. Are you _____ about that?

b. Without health _____, you may not be able to pay all
   your medical bills.

c. Have you ever swum in the _____?

d. The coffee from the coffee _____ tastes terrible!

Now remember all the different words you've studied with the "SH" sound.

PROOFREAD

If the sentence is correct, write *OK*. If a word is misspelled, cross out the word and write it correctly on the line.

a. This necklace has preshus stones. _____

b. Permission was granted. _____

c. He took out a new inshurance policy. _____

d. He is an efficient worker. _____

e. They're having finantial problems. _____

f. Would you like to work for a big corporasion? _____

g. This pie is delishus! _____

h. Can you fix this washing mashine? _____

i. The plane flew over the ocean. _____

j. My physition prescribed a new drug. _____

Answers start on page 123.

Special Consonant Sounds 4: "CH" Sound

WORDS TO KNOW

*actually   *naturally

*amateur   *signature

*future   *temperature

*manufacture   *unnatural

And now meet the **future** heavyweight **champion!**

Read the sentence above out loud and notice the "CH" sound in the bold-type words.

Guide: The "CH" sound is spelled with the letters *ch* in short words and at the beginnings of words (*champion*). It is often spelled with the letters *tu* in the middle of longer words (*future*).

Circle the *tu* in each word, and do the Say-Copy-Check exercise:

*actually _____   *signature _____

*future _____   *temperature _____

*manufacture _____   *unnatural _____

*naturally _____

In one special spelling, the "CH" sound is spelled with *teu*. Circle *teu* and do the Say-Copy-Check exercise:

*amateur _____

PRACTICE

Fill in the correct *tu* (or *teu*) word with the "CH" sound.

a. He _____ ate five hamburgers!

b. Tell me about your plans for the _____.

c. Put your _____ next to the X.

d. The normal body _____ is 98.6 degrees Fahrenheit.

e. Green is an _____ hair color.

f. Recently, the _____ of steel has declined.

g. My brother is an _____ photographer.

Answers start on page 123.

Special Consonant Sounds 5: "ZH" Sound

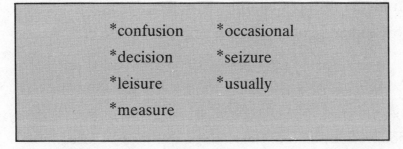

WORDS
TO
KNOW

*confusion   *occasional

*decision   *seizure

*leisure   *usually

*measure

She **usually** makes a **decision** and sticks to it.

Say the sentence above out loud and listen to the "ZH" sound in the bold-type words.

> **Guide:** The "ZH" sound is usually written with *sion* or *su*.

SION Combination

Circle *sion* and do the Say-Copy-Check exercise:

*confusion _____

*decision _____

*occasional _____

Note that *sion* sounds like "ZH," as in *deciSION,* and *ssion* sounds like "SH," as in *miSSION*. Don't confuse the two endings.

SU Combination

Circle *su* and do the Say-Copy-Check exercise:

*leisure _____

*measure _____

*usually _____

In one case, *zu* is used instead of *su*. Circle the *zu* and do the Say-Copy-Check exercise.

*seizure _____

Fill in the missing words that have the "ZH" sound.

a. People _____ eat lunch around noon.

b. I'm not changing my mind. My _____ is final.

c. They put him in the hospital when he had a _____.

d. Would you rather be busy all the time or lead a life of _____?

e. You need to _____ your living room before you order carpeting.

f. The announcement did not clear things up—it just caused more _____.

g. She makes an _____ error, but usually her work is excellent.

Answers start on page 123.

Special Consonant Sounds 6: "J" Sound

WORDS TO KNOW

*apologize	*genuine	*schedule
*education	*gradually	*soldier
*general	*individual	*tragedy
*generous	*procedure	*vegetable

The **jet** pilot prevented a **tragedy** by following the correct **emergency procedure.**

Read the sentence above out loud and notice the "J" sound in the bold-type words.

Guide: In short words (*jet*), *j* is used to spell the "J" sound. In longer words, *ge, gi,* and *du* spell this sound (*tragedy, procedure*).

GE/GI Combinations

Before *e* and *i, g* usually sounds like "J." Circle the *ge* or *gi* in each word. Then do the Say-Copy-Check exercise, capitalizing *ge* or *gi* the first time you copy the word.

*apologize _____

*general _____

*generous _____

*genuine _____

*tragedy _____

*vegetable _____

———————————— **PRACTICE 1** ————————————

Fill in the missing *ge* or *gi* words that you've studied.

a. not specific: _____

b. not stingy: _____

c. a kind of food: _____

d. say "I'm sorry": _____

e. real: _____

f. terrible event: _____

DU Combination

Sometimes *du* sounds like "J." Circle the *du* in these words and do the Say-Copy-Check exercise.

*education _____   *procedure _____

*gradually _____   *schedule _____

*individual _____

One word spells the "J" sound with *di*. Circle *di* and do the Say-Copy-Check exercise:

*soldier _____

Another spelling for the "J" sound is *dg* as in badge. Circle *dg* and do the Say-Copy-Check exercise:

*judgment _____

PRACTICE 2

Fill in the missing *du* (or *di*) words.

A _____ in the army receives a different
                  a

_____ than he got in high school. He must follow a rigorous
          b

_____—getting up at the crack of dawn and working hard all
          c

day. He must learn to follow every military _____ to the
                                                              d

letter. _____, he learns to forget his own
              e

_____ needs and to think of himself as a member of a team.
          f

Remember all of the ways to spell the "J" sound as you do the next exercise.

PROOFREAD

If the sentence is correct, write *OK*. If there is a misspelled word, cross out the word and spell it correctly on the line.

a. You are very jenerous. _____

b. It was a terrible tragedy. _____

c. The solger was killed in action. _____

d. What's your new schejule? _____

e. This is genuine leather. _____

f. Have some vejetable soup. _____

g. What is the correct preceger to follow? _____

h. Her hair gradually turned gray. _____

i. They come in individgual wrappers. _____

Answers start on page 123.

18

Special Consonant Sounds 7: "F" Sound

WORDS TO KNOW	*cough	*financial	*pamphlet	*physical
	*enough	*nephew	*philosophy	*physician
	*future	*official	*phobia	*telephone

You've made **enough** long-distance **telephone** calls to destroy our **financial** security!

Read the sentence above out loud and notice the "F" sound in the bold-type words.

> **Guide:** The "F" sound is usually spelled with *f* or *ff* (*financial, official*). *Ph* and *gh* are sometimes used to spell this sound (*telephone, enough*).

PH Combination

A number of common words use *ph* instead of *f*. Circle the *ph* and do the Say-Copy-Check exercise:

*nephew _____   *physical _____

*pamphlet _____   *physician _____

*philosophy _____   *telephone _____

*phobia _____

PRACTICE 1

Fill in the missing *ph* words.

a. doctor: _____

b. not mental: _____

c. niece's brother: _____

d. brochure or flyer: _____

e. communication instrument: _____

f. unreasonable fear: _____

g. belief system: _____

GH Combination

In a few words, *gh* is used instead of *f*. Circle the *gh* and do the Say-Copy-Check exercise:

*cough _____   rough _____

*enough _____   tough _____

laugh _____

Complete each sentence with the correct *gh* word.

a. This meat is too _____.

b. The opposite of smooth is _____.

c. Don't _____! It's not funny.

d. I don't have _____ time to watch TV.

e. Cover your mouth when you _____.

Remember all the words you've studied with the "F" sound as you do the next exercise.

PROOFREAD

Cross out the misspelled word and write it correctly on the line.

a. future   fobia   farm   _____

b. puff   enuff   cuff   _____

c. knife   few   nefew   _____

d. filosophy   financial   telephone   _____

e. official   final   fisician   _____

f. phly   physical   phone   _____

Answers start on page 123.

Special Consonant Sounds 8: "K" Sound

WORDS TO KNOW	*ache *bouquet *character *liquor	*mechanic *psychiatrist *psychologist *schedule	*school *technique *technology

The **mechanic** will **keep** your **car** for a few days so he **can** try a new repair **technique** on it.

Read the sentence above out loud and notice the spelling of the "K" sound.

Guide: *K* is sometimes used to spell the "K" sound in short words (*keep*), but the letter *c* is more commonly used to spell this sound in both short and long words (*car, careful*). Two other spellings sometimes used for the "K" sound are *ch* and *qu* (*mechanic, technique*).

CH Combination

Circle the *ch* and do the Say-Copy-Check exercise, capitalizing the *ch* the first time you copy the word.

*ache _____

*character _____

*mechanic _____

*psychiatrist _____

*psychologist _____

*schedule _____

*school _____

*stomach _____

*technique _____

*technology _____

Here are some spelling tricks to help you recall the *ch* in some of these words. Fill in the missing letters and then copy the tricks into your notebook.

sCHool sCHedule	s____ool s____edule
sCHool psyCHologist	s____ool psy____ologist
sCHool for meCHanics	s____ool for me____anics

21

QU Combination

Circle the *qu* and do the Say-Copy-Check exercise:

antique _____

*bouquet _____

*liquor _____

*technique _____

Keep in mind the different *ch* and *qu* spellings for the "K" sound as you do the next exercise.

PROOFREAD ————

Find and correct the eight errors in the paragraph below. The first one has been done for you.

> *psychologist*
>
> Dr. Sonya Biggs is a ~~psycologist~~ at Denter High Shool, where she has a very busy scedule. Although few students have real caracter disorders, there are many students who have less serious psycological problems. Some students abuse drugs or ligor, and Dr. Biggs uses a variety of tecnicues to treat them. Other students have problems at home. Even though Dr. Biggs often goes home with a headake, she wouldn't give up her work for the world.

Answers start on page 123.

Looking Up Spellings

You've just studied different ways to spell certain sounds, and you've learned words with these spellings. But they aren't the only words in the English language with special spellings. What if there's a word you need to spell that you haven't studied before? Let's say you have written this sentence:

I'm interested in m..............l arts, like karate and kung fu.

There is one word you don't know how to spell. Time to give up? No. If you use your dictionary along with what you already know about spelling, you'll be able to find the right spelling of this word. First think—how could you possibly spell the word? There are several ways to spell the "SH" sound. Take out your pencil and write down all the possibilities:

marshal   marcial   martial

All three spellings are possible **in theory,** but which is **right?** Maybe you can tell just by looking—your eyes will often recognize the right word. If not, grab your dictionary and check each possibility. If we go in alphabetical order, we'll start with *marcial.* Find the right page by looking at the guide words. You'd see something like this:

march -------------
----
mar·chion·ess ----------------

Mar·di Gras -----------

The spelling *marcial* is not even in the dictionary! If it had been, you would have found it between **marchioness** and **Mardi Gras.** Now we can forget that attempt at the word.

Try the next possibility: *marshal.* This word you **will** find, but look at the definition:

mar·shal *n.* 1. In some countries, a military officer of the highest rank. 2. An official in charge of a ceremony. *v.* 1. To arrange in order. 2. To guide.

At first glance, this seems to be the right word—after all, the definition *is* related to the military. But when we talk about karate and kung fu, are we really talking about an officer or arranging in order? Let's check the third spelling possibility to make sure. Here's what you'd find:

mar·tial *adj.* 1. Of or related to war or warriors 2. military

That's more like it! Karate and kung fu are *military* and are related to *warriors,* so this must be the right word. The word we're looking for is **martial**—*martial arts!*

Let's go through the steps of figuring out how to spell a word:

1. Write down all the reasonable possible spellings. (Use your knowledge of spelling rules and guidelines.)
2. If you can't tell which possibility is correct by looking, look up each in the dictionary.
3. If it's not in the dictionary, you can probably forget this possibility.
4. If it's in the dictionary, check the definition to be sure it's really the word you want. If the definition fits, you've got your word!

In each sentence, there is a missing word. To the right are listed two or three possible spellings for that word. Use your own dictionary to decide which is correct. Write the correct word on the line.

a. It was a _____ development. (mager majer major)

b. The farmer put animal chow in the pig _____.

   (troff troph trough)

c. He likes to _____ at 7:00. (arise arize)

d. There was a fly on the _____. (cealing ceiling sealing)

e. Our VCR gives us a lot of _____. (pleasure pleazure)

f. She has a soft, _____ touch. (gentile gentle jentle)

g. She has a _____ case of bronchitis.

   (cronic chronic kronic)

h. There is a certain _____ about her.

   (mysteek mysteke mystique)

i. The dentist said he had too much _____ on his teeth.

   (plac plack plaque)

j. They were poisoned by the deadly _____.

   (tocsin toxin)

k. The children played in the _____. (alley ally)

l. When he took the drug, he started to _____.

   (hallusinate hallucinate)

Answers start on page 123.

Double Consonants

WORDS
TO
KNOW

*aggressive	*dilemma	*interrupt	*sufficient
*agree	*dollar	*message	*summary
*allow	*efficient	*necessary	*terrible
*annual	*embarrass	*official	*tobacco
*baggage	*exaggerate	*omit	*tomorrow
*balloon	*fulfillment	*parallel	*valley
*bottom	*gimmick	*possession	
*bulletin	*grammar	*possible	
*career	*happen	*professor	
*cigarette	*horrible	*quarrel	
*different	*intelligent	*stubborn	

baGGage   tomoRRow   embaRRaSS

Double consonants are a common sight in English. Sometimes they result from attaching prefixes or suffixes to words. Sometimes they are the result of other factors in the history of our language.

In this section, you'll study often-misspelled words with double letters. If you can master these sometimes troublesome words, you will see a noticeable improvement in your spelling.

FF Words

To remember the *ff* in these words, first say the beginning out loud. Then circle the *ff* and do the Say-Copy-Check exercise.

DIFF—*different _____   OFF—*official _____

EFF—*efficient _____   SUFF—*sufficient _____

PRACTICE

Fill in the opposite of each word. Choose from the *ff* words above.

a. same: _____

b. lacking: _____

c. informal: _____

d. slow: _____

GG Words

To remember the *gg* in these words, say the beginning out loud. Then circle the *gg* and do the Say-Copy-Check exercise.

AGG—*aggressive _____   BAGG—*baggage _____

In the next word, *agg* sounds like "AJ." Circle the *agg* and do the Say-Copy-Check exercise.

*exaggerate _____

When you say this word, put extra stress on the two *g*s. Say exagggggerate." In other words, *exaggerate* the *g*s in *exaggerate*. This will help you remember the correct spelling.

NOTE: Watch out for the word *agree*. It has only one *g*. Circle the *g* and do the Say-Copy-Check exercise.

*agree _____

Write a sentence with this word in your notebook.

LL Words

To remember the *ll* in these words, say the beginning out loud. Then circle the *ll* in these words and do the Say-Copy-Check exercise.

ALL—*allow _____   FILL—*fulfillment _____

BALL—*balloon _____   TELL—*intelligent _____

BULL—*bulletin _____   VALL—*valley _____

DOLL—*dollar _____

Write spelling tricks for some of the *ll* words and then copy them into your notebook.

     a. fulfillment (Hint: Use *fill*.) *I want to FILL my life with fulFILLment.*

     b. allow (Hint: Use *all*.) _____

     c. balloon (Hint: Use *ball*.) _____

     d. bulletin (Hint: Use *bull*.) _____

     e. intelligent (Hint: Use *tell*.) _____

There is one more double-*l* word that is tricky. Circle *all* and do the Say-Copy-Check exercise.

*parallel _____

Here is a spelling trick. Imagine a town with eleven streets:

ALL ELeven streets are *parALLEL.*

Fill in the missing letters and copy the trick into your notebook.

_____ ____even streets are par_____.

Fill in the missing *ll* word.

a. We used to live high in the mountains, but now we live down in the

_____.

b. I wish I had a dime for every _____ I've spent.

c. She wants to go to the party, but her father won't _____

it.

d. He gets good grades. He is very _____.

e. Getting a high school diploma was the _____ of her

lifelong goal.

f. The clown had a big bunch of red, green, and orange

_____.

MM Words

For these words, say "mmmmmm" and repeat the words and word parts written below. Then copy each word into your notebook.

MMMM—LEMMA—*dilemma _____

MMMM—GIMM—*gimmick _____

MMMM—GRAMM—*grammar _____

MMMM—SUMM—*summary _____

Here are some spelling tricks to help you remember some of these *mm* words. Fill in the missing letters and then copy them into your notebook.

EMMA has a *dilEMMA.*

_____ has a dil_____.

In *SUMMARY,* what's the *SUM, MARY?*

In _____, what's the _____, _____?

NOTE: The word *omit* has only one *m.* Circle the *m* and do the Say-Copy-Check exercise.

*omit _____

Write a sentence with *omit* in your notebook.

Fill in the missing *mm* word.

a. The teacher gave a _____ of the book.

b. Her son writes well and he is very good at English _____.

c. The judge was on the horns of a _____.

d. If they are giving away free merchandise, you can be sure there is a

_____ to it.

RR Words

To remember the *rr* in these words, say the word parts out loud and then say the entire word. Circle the *rr* and do the Say-Copy-Check exercise.

BARR—*embarrass _____   QUARR—*quarrel _____

ORR—*horrible _____   TERR—*terrible _____

Remember this easy spelling trick:

A *teRRible, hoRRible, embaRRassing, quaRRel*

Copy it into your notebook.

Another difficult word is *tomorrow*. To remember the spelling, first think of the word *today* and then separate the parts of these words:

to day: today   to morrow: tomorrow

Now imagine that *Morrow* is the name of a town. Here's a spelling trick:

They're going *TO MORROW TOMORROW*.

Copy this trick into your notebook.

For the last word, *interrupt*, imagine a line *interrupting* the word:

inter | rupt

If you can remember the line as *interrupting* the two *r*s, you'll remember to write them.

Circle the *rr* and do the Say-Copy-Check exercise:

*interrupt _____

========== PRACTICE ==========

Fill in the missing *rr* words.

a. She's so mean that we call her _____ Harriet.

b. My baby has reached "the _____ twos."

c. I can't go today. How about _____?

d. Please don't _____ me. Let me finish.

e. Mr. and Mrs. Moss never _____. They are very happy together.

f. Why do you always _____ me in public?

NOTE: The word *career* has only one *r* in the middle. Circle the first *r* and do the Say-Copy-Check exercise:

*career _____

Write a sentence with *career* in your notebook.

SS Words

To remember the *ss,* say the word parts out loud and then say the words. Circle the *ss* and do the Say-Copy-Check exercise.

CESS—*necessary _____

FESS—*professor _____

MESS—*message _____

POSS—*possession _____

POSS—*possible _____

To remember the spelling of *professor,* think of the word in three parts: *pro fess or.* Can you write a spelling trick for *professor?* (Hint: Use *confess.*)

_____

And remember the spelling trick for *necessary:*

CESSA says it's ne*CESSA*ry.

──────────────── PRACTICE ────────────────

Fill in the missing *ss* word.

a. All things are _____, if you only believe.

b. My _____ is a top-notch instructor.

c. I took a telephone _____ for you.

d. It's against the law to have a gun in your _____.

Other Double Letters

Here are some other words with various double letters. Circle the double letters and do the Say-Copy-Check exercise.

*annual _____

*bottom _____

*cigarette _____

*happen _____

*stubborn _____

*tobacco _____

Note that *cigarette* is really *cigar* + *ette.* The *-ette* comes from French and means "little," so we're really saying "little cigar." You can see *-ette* in some women's names, like Annette and Yvette.

Now write spelling tricks for some of these words.

a. stubborn (Hint: Use *Tubbo*.) _____

b. cigarette (Hint: Use the name *Yvette*.) _____

c. annual (Hint: Use the name *Ann*.) _____

d. happen (Hint: Use *happy*.) _____

e. bottom (Hint: Use the name *Otto*.) _____

Now try to remember all the words you've studied with double consonants.

PROOFREAD

Cross out the misspelled word and write it correctly on the line.

a. agressive   sufficient   difference   _____

b. possible   terrible   embarass   _____

c. ciggarete   baggage   bottom   _____

d. dilemma   tommorow   horrible   _____

e. dollar   balloon   bulettin   _____

f. fullfilment   parallel   allow   _____

g. sufficient   proffesor   message   _____

h. neccesary   exaggerate   possession   _____

CROSSWORD PUZZLE

Many of the words in this puzzle are ones you've studied in this chapter. They are marked with an asterisk (*).

ACROSS

*1. opposite of passive

*8. luggage

11. _____ constrictor (snake)

*12. complete satisfaction: _____ ment

13. another name for the crime syndicate: the _____

*14. a hard choice

15. weep

16. past tense of *eat*

18. safety _____

19. place to see animals

20. to mail

*22. yearly

23. not no

24. hello

*26. lets

*27. occur

DOWN

*2. Your instructor wants you to use good spelling and _____.

*3. enough

*4. something you find between mountains

*5. There's a notice on the _____ board.

6. steal

7. Ma and _____

*8. You'll find these at birthday parties.

*9. Oh, that's just a sales _____!

*10. to shame

14. the way you feel if you're standing on top of a building looking down

16. monkey

17. not the beginning

20. hit

21. sound a cow makes

24. _____ and she

25. not out

Answers start on page 123.

Silent Consonants

WORDS TO KNOW				
*acknowledge	*eight	*height	*mortgage	*rhythm
*answer	*eighth	*heir	*plumber	*solemn
*autumn	*exhausted	*honor	*psalm	*straight
*calm	*exhibit	*knee	*psychiatrist	*subtle
*campaign	*fasten	*knife	*psychological	*undoubtedly
*debt	*fatigue	*knob	*psychologist	*Wednesday
*delight	*February	*knot	*receipt	*wrap
		*knowledge	*rhyme	*wring

He is **eight** hundred dollars in **debt**.

Read the sentence above out loud and note the silent *gh* in *eight* and the silent *b* in *debt*. There are a number of other words that, like *eight* and *debt*, have silent consonants. Work through the following exercises to learn these words.

"Silent B"

Circle the "silent B" and do the Say-Copy-Check exercise.

*debt _____

doubt _____

*plumber _____

*subtle _____

*undoubtedly _____

—————————————— PRACTICE ——————————————

Read the definitions and fill in the missing words with the "silent B."

a. money owed: _____

b. pipe worker: _____

c. not obvious: _____

d. unsureness: _____

e. unquestionably: _____

"Silent GH"

The combination *gh* is often silent. *Gh* frequently follows the letter *i*. Circle the *gh* in each word and do the Say-Copy-Check exercise.

*delight _____   *height _____

*eight _____   *straight _____

*eighth _____   tonight _____

━━━━━━━━━━━━━━━━━━━━━━━ PRACTICE ━━━━━━━━━━━━━━━━━━━━━━━

Read the definitions and fill in the correct "silent GH" words.

a. great happiness: _____

b. tallness: _____

c. this evening: _____

d. not curly: _____

e. after seven: _____

f. after seventh: _____

"Silent H"

Circle the "silent H" in these words and do the Say-Copy-Check exercise.

*exhausted _____   *honor _____

*exhibit _____   *rhyme _____

*heir _____   *rhythm _____

━━━━━━━━━━━━━━━━━━━━━━━ PRACTICE ━━━━━━━━━━━━━━━━━━━━━━━

Fill in the missing "silent H" words.

a. It is an _____ to meet you, sir.

b. Did you see the new art _____?

c. In a poem, certain words _____ with each other.

d. He is _____ to a great fortune.

e. I can't dance. I have no sense of _____.

f. After working ten straight hours, I am totally _____.

"Silent K"

K is often silent in the combination *kn*. Circle *kn* and do the Say-Copy-Check exercise.

*knee _____   *knob _____   *knowledge _____

*knife _____   *knot _____

One way to remember the *k* in spelling these words is to mispronounce them on purpose. Say, for example, "ka-nee" for *knee*. This way, you'll remember to write the *k*. *(Of course, you should do this only as you're trying to learn the words! Don't mispronounce them in everyday speech.)*

Fill in the missing words with the "silent K."

Kirby was the only living man with the _____ of the
a

secret formula, and now he was caught—tied up in a hidden room. He tried

to undo the _____ around his wrists, but it was impossible.
b

Suddenly, he saw the door _____ turn. The door opened,
c

and in crept Celia, the woman who had helped capture him. "I've fallen in

love with you," she said. Then she got down on one _____
d

and cut his ropes with a _____, and the two escaped
e

together.

"Silent P"

P is silent at the beginning of many words that come from the Greek language. All of the words
start with the "S" sound, and the *p* is part of the letter combination *ps*. Circle the *ps* and do the
Say-Copy-Check exercise.

*psalm _____   *psychological _____

*psychiatrist _____   *psychologist _____

P is also silent in the following word. Circle the *p* and do the Say-Copy-Check exercise.

*receipt _____

Here is a spelling trick to help you remember the *p* in *receipt:*

KeeP the receiPt when you receive it.

Fill in the missing letters and then write the trick in your notebook.

Kee__ the recei__t when you receive it.

Look at the clues in parentheses and fill in the missing words with the "silent
P."

a. The minister recited the twenty-third _____. (—alm)

b. She was a child _____. (—ychologist)

c. She conducted a _____ experiment. (—ychological)

d. He went to a _____ because he had some problems to
work out. (—ychiatrist)

e. Do you need a _____? (rece—)

34

"Silent W"

Circle the "silent W" and do the Say-Copy-Check exercise.

*acknowledge _____   *wrap _____

*answer _____   *wring _____

―――――――――――――――――――――― PRACTICE ――――――――――――――――――――――

Fill in the missing "silent W" words.

a. _____ up the package.

b. _____ my question!

c. _____ all the water out of the wet bathing suits.

d. He refused to _____ my presence.

Other Silent Consonants

Various other consonants are silent in some words. Find and circle the silent consonant in each of the following words and then do the Say-Copy-Check exercise. Capitalize the silent consonant the first time you copy it.

*autumn _____   *February _____

*calm _____   *mortgage _____

*campaign _____   *solemn _____

*fasten _____   *Wednesday _____

NOTE: The first *r* in *February* is not a silent consonant, however it is frequently not pronounced.

Here are some spelling tricks. Fill in the missing letters and then copy the tricks into your notebook.

The *WEDding* is *NExt WEDNEsday.*   *MorT got a morTgage.*

The _____ding is _____xt _____sday.   *Mor__ got a mor__gage.*

Once again, pronouncing a word as it looks—Wed-nes-day or mort-gage—will help you learn how to spell it correctly.

―――――――――――――――――――――― PRACTICE ――――――――――――――――――――――

Write the missing words with the silent consonants you've just studied.

a. Another word for the season fall is _____.

b. The second month of the year is _____.

c. _____ your seat belts.

d. It was a _____ occasion; no one smiled at all.

e. Don't panic. Try to remain _____.

f. The president has begun his _____ for reelection.

g. The class meets on Monday, _____, and Friday.

Answers start on page 124.

Review of Consonants

In this exercise, write OK if the sentence is correct. If a word is misspelled, cross it out and write it correctly on the line. Be careful! Some of the answers contain silent or double consonants.

a. I'll see you tommorrow. _____

b. It takes discipline to be a good athlete. _____

c. I've had enuf of this garbage. _____

d. What is the anser to the question? _____

e. Gold is a precious metal. _____

f. How much morgage do you owe on your house? _____

g. The day after Tuesday is Wensday. _____

h. It will be necesary to move him to a hospital if he continues bleeding. _____

i. It was so foggy outside the road was barely visible. _____

j. We'll have to analyse the situation before we make a recommendation. _____

k. Dexter is an associate of mine. _____

l. Please affix your signachure on the dotted line. _____

m. Her father is in the hospital; he suffered a seizhure. _____

n. Is this the correct procedjure? _____

o. Let's get fhysical! Fhysical! _____

p. The mekanik is changing my oil. _____

q. Don't drink licker before driving an automobile. _____

r. The two ceiling beams are parallel to one another. _____

s. I will acknoledge your letter as soon as possible. _____

t. She has a sychological problem! _____

u. He has really grown in height over the past year. _____

v. Remember to get a receit! _____

w. The street we live on is very strait and narrow. _____

Answers start on page 124.

A Letter of Thanks

An important part of any job search is an interview. Afterwards, it is advisable to send the interviewer a thank you letter. This is not only a matter of courtesy; it is also a way to show your interest in the job and to keep your name in the person's mind.

Here are some useful words for your letter. Copy each into your notebook.

USEFUL WORDS

Verbs	Nouns		Adjectives
appreciate	appreciation	interview	eager
contact	attention	*opportunity	*further
hesitate	information	*personnel	grateful
provide	*interest		interested
			pleased

PROOFREAD

Lisa Wolek was interviewed at the Seaview Bank and wrote a letter of thanks. Help her find and correct the eleven spelling errors. (Don't forget to check the words at the top!)

161 Esperanza Dr.

San Diego, CA 92120

Mrs. Estela Herrera

Personel Director

Seaview Bank

1400 Ridgeway Rd.

San Diego, CA 92136

Dear Mrs. Herrera:

I would like to express my apreciation for the oportunity you gave me to learn more about the teller position at Seaview Bank and to tell you about my own background. After the intervue, my intrest in working at your bank is even stronger than before.

If I can pervide any farther infomation about my qualifications, please do not hestate to contac me.

Again, thank you for your time and atention.

Sincerely,

Lisa Wolek

Lisa Wolek

Answers start on page 124.

Sounds to Spell

    Silent Vowels

    Reduced Vowel Roots

    Reduced Vowel Suffixes

Words for Now

    Letter to a School

Words to Use

    Past Tense and Past Participles

Dictionary Exercise

    Finding Difficult Past Forms

    and Past Participles

SOUNDS TO SPELL

Silent Vowels

WORDS TO KNOW				
*build	*fashion	*guidance	*jealous	*nuisance
*carriage	*guarantee	*guitar	*marriage	*theory
*diamond				

After his **marrIage,** he became **jeAlous** of his wife's **frIends.**

In the sentence above, notice that each boldface word has a silent vowel. Through the evolution of our language, some sounds have been lost from our pronunciation, but the letters remain in our spelling. For this reason, it's easy to forget to write these silent letters. Work through the following exercises to make sure **you** won't forget the silent letters.

"Silent A"

The combination *ea* is often pronounced like "short E"; the *a* is silent. You already know short words with this combination, like *head, breath,* and *heavy.* Here are three longer words to learn. Say each out loud. Then circle the *ea* and do the Say-Copy-Check exercise.

*jealous _____

*measure _____

*pleasant _____

The combination *ia* sometimes sounds like "long I"; again, the *a* is silent. Circle the *a* in the words below and copy them once each.

dial _____

*diamond _____

Fill in the correct words with the "silent A," using the combination *ea* or *ia*.

a. Did you have a _____ evening?

b. The car didn't _____ up to our expectations.

c. She has a _____ ring.

d. Are you _____ of people with a lot of money?

e. Pick up the phone and _____ 555–1234.

"Silent I"

The letter *i* is silent in some words. Say each word below out loud and circle the "silent I." Then do the Say-Copy-Check exercise, capitalizing the *i* the first time you copy the word.

*carriage _____   *marriage _____

*fashion _____   *nuisance _____

Fill in the correct words with the "silent I."

a. Their _____ lasted only two years.

b. She is a _____ designer.

c. Don't be such a _____!

d. Put the baby in the baby _____.

"Silent U"

"Silent U" often appears after *g* to keep the "hard G" sound before *i* or *e*. Circle *gu* and do the Say-Copy-Check exercise.

*fatigue _____   *guidance _____

*guarantee _____   *guitar _____

"Silent U" also appears in the next word. Circle the *u* and do the Say-Copy-Check exercise.

*build _____

Fill in the missing "silent U" words.

a. Can you play the _____?

b. They're going to _____ a house here.

c. Children need strong _____.

d. The _____ showed in her face.

e. This product has a money-back _____.

"Silent O"

Two common words have the "silent O." Circle the *o* and do the Say-Copy-Check exercise.

people _____

*theory _____

Here is a spelling trick:

The *peOple* have an *Odd theOry*.

Fill in the missing letters and then write the trick in your notebook.

The pe__ple have an __dd the__ry.

As you do the following exercises, keep in mind everything you've learned about words with silent letters.

PROOFREAD ———

The exercise below contains words with both silent vowels and silent consonants. If the sentence is correct, write *OK*. If a word is misspelled, cross it out and write it correctly on the line.

a. He looked strate ahead. _____

b. Wring out the wet dish towel. _____

c. I'll see you on Wendesday. _____

d. The plummer fixed our sink. _____

e. It's a nuisance to take out the garbage. _____

f. He made a solemm pledge. _____

g. He has sychological problems. _____

h. She has shared her knowledge with all of us. _____

i. They are undoutedly surprised at the results. _____

j. Her birthday is Feburary 23. _____

k. He tied a not in his shoelace. _____

l. She's just suffering from fatigue. _____

m. The pilot told us to fassen our seat belts. _____

n. The politicians agreed to conduct a clean campain. _____

o. Marla sang, and Elliott played the gitar. _____

p. Which is more important—love or honor? _____

q. The band has a large rythm section. _____

r. There is a suttle difference between these two shades of pink. _____

s. They are deeply in debt. _____

Letter to a School

Someday soon, you may decide you need more education or training to reach your career goal. You may have to write a letter to a college or other school requesting information about its programs. Your spelling will certainly make an impression on the director of admissions. Below are listed some words that will be useful in writing your letter. Copy them carefully into your notebook.

USEFUL WORDS

*admission	certificate	curriculum	graduate
application	*college	dean	*interest
*appropriate	*community	degree	program
assistance	*computer	*eligible	*schedule
catalogue	courses	*financial	

PROOFREAD

Ms. Lovett wrote a good letter—with the exception of her spelling! Find and correct the twenty errors. The first one has been done for you.

Ms. Alma L. Robinson

Director of Ad~~missions~~ *Admissions*

Fordham Comunity Colege

8300 Lynn Pl.

Colonia, NJ 07067

Dear Ms. Robinson:

I am a recent GED gradduate seeking information regarding admission to your air conditioning and refrigeration pogram. I also have an intrest in the electronics and computor certificites offered through your colege and am anxious to know more about your curiculum. Would it be possible to have a scedule of fall corses, a catelogue, and an aplication form sent to me?

I spoke with the deane last week, and he indicated that since I am a veteran and will be a deggree-seeking student I would be elgible for finantial assistence. Please send me the appropiate form to apply for this aid.

Thank you for your attention.

Sincerely,

Carrie Lovett

Carrie Lovett

Answers start on page 124.

Spelling that Doesn't Match the Pronunciation

WORDS TO KNOW

*again	*bureau	*courteous	*machine	*technique
*against	*business	*fatigue	*maneuver	*tongue
*anxious	*busy	*foreign	*neutral	*trouble
*beautiful	*country	*gasoline	*recipe	*vacuum
*bouquet	*courage	*gauge	*sergeant	*young
			*souvenir	

He's having trubble with his bizniss.

Can you spot the two misspelled words in the sentence above? The spellings *trubble* and *bizniss* accurately reflect the words' pronunciation, but, in fact, they are *not* correct spellings. Instead of *trubble* and *bizniss,* the words should be spelled **trouble** and **business.** *Trouble* and *business* are hard words because their spelling does not reflect their pronunciation.

There are a number of words, like these, whose spellings don't match their pronunciation. In some cases, the words used to be pronounced differently in the past. Then the pronunciation changed, but the spelling stayed the same. In other cases, the words are imported from other languages with different spelling systems. In any case, you'll need to memorize these tricky words.

Words with Unusual Vowel Spellings

Most people say the "short E" or "short I" sound in the words *again* and *against.* To remember the *ai* spelling, think of this spelling trick:

He made *A GAIN, AGAIN.*

Fill in the missing words and then copy the trick into your notebook.

He made ___ _____, _____.

Then remember that *against = again + st.* Now circle the *ai* and do the Say-Copy-Check exercise.

*again _____   *against _____

──────────── PRACTICE 1 ────────────

Fill in *again* or *against* correctly.

a. He leaned _____ the wall.

b. She got sick _____.

c. We had to start all over _____.

d. Are you for or _____ the death penalty?

42

You hear the "short I" and the "Z" sound in the words *business* and *busy*. Circle the *us* in each word and do the Say-Copy-Check exercise.

*business _____   *busy _____

Now write a sentence with each word.

_____

_____

The "short U" sound in the words below is spelled with the letter *o* or the combination *ou*. Circle the *o* or *ou* in these words and do the Say-Copy-Check exercise.

*country _____   *trouble _____

*tongue _____   *young _____

━━━━━━━━━━━━━━━━━ PRACTICE 2 ━━━━━━━━━━━━━━━━━

Fill in the correct words with the "short U" sound.

a. He is too _____ to drive.

b. Canada is a large _____ .

c. Stick out your _____ .

d. Are you having _____ with the homework?

You can hear the "long U" in the words *maneuver* and *neutral*, even though they are spelled with *eu*. Circle the *eu* and do the Say-Copy-Check exercise.

*maneuver _____   *neutral _____

━━━━━━━━━━━━━━━━━ PRACTICE 3 ━━━━━━━━━━━━━━━━━

Fill in the missing words with *eu*.

a. The ships will practice a new _____ in the gulf.

b. I cannot take sides on this issue. I am _____ .

In the next words, you don't hear a clear vowel sound. *Cour* sounds like "KER." Circle the *cour* and do the Say-Copy-Check exercise.

*courage _____ .

*courteous _____

Write a sentence with each word:

_____

_____

Words from French

A number of words come to us directly or indirectly from French. Notice the *eau* combination in these words. It's pronounced in different ways. Circle *eau* and do the Say-Copy-Check exercise.

*beautiful _____   *bureau _____

beauty _____   bureaucracy _____

━━━━━━━━━━━━━━ PRACTICE 1 ━━━━━━━━━━━━━━

Fill in the correct words with *eau*.

a. This newspaper has a London _____.

b. Her _____ is beyond compare.

c. You are simply _____.

d. This government _____ is so complicated.

In the next words, the letter *i* is used where you hear the "long E" sound. Circle the *i* and do the Say-Copy-Check exercise.

*fatigue _____   *machine _____

*gasoline _____   *technique _____

In the following word, the letter *i* sounds like "long E" or "short I." Circle the *i* and do the Say-Copy-Check exercise.

*souvenir _____

━━━━━━━━━━━━━━ PRACTICE 2 ━━━━━━━━━━━━━━

Fill in the correct word with the letter *i*.

a. This ashtray is a _____ of Niagara Falls.

b. The doctor tried a new surgical _____.

c. This car takes only unleaded _____.

d. This soft drink _____ is out of order.

e. The _____ was visible in her weary eyes.

You can hear the "long A" sound in the next two words. In *bouquet,* the *quet* sounds like "KAY." Circle the *quet* and do the Say-Copy-Check exercise.

*bouquet _____

In *gauge,* the *au* sounds like "AY." Circle the *au* and do the Say-Copy-Check exercise.

*gauge _____

Fill in the correct words with the "long A" sound.

a. Remember to check the gas _____.

b. He gave her a _____ of flowers.

The next word sounds like "sargent" but is spelled *sergeant*. Do the Say-Copy-Check exercise.

*sergeant _____

Write a sentence with this word.

_____

Other Difficult Spellings

Several other words have spellings that do not match their pronunciation. Look at the incorrect spellings on the left; then find the correct spelling on the right, and do the Say-Copy-Check exercise.

ressuppee   *anxious _____

ankshus   *foreign _____

vackyoom   *vacuum _____

forrin   *recipe _____

━━━━━━━━━━━━━━━━━━━ **PRACTICE** ━━━━━━━━━━━━━━━━━━━

Fill in the correct words.

a. He traveled to many _____ lands.

b. We need a new _____ cleaner.

c. I am very _____ about my son's performance at school.

d. Could I have the _____ for these delicious brownies?

Now keep in mind the words with unusual spellings as you do the following exercises.

WORD GAMES ━━━━━━

Scrambled Words
Unscramble the words below. The first one has been done for you.

a. NAGIA ____AGAIN____

b. CERIPE _____

c. CUVAMU _____

d. SUBY _____

e. GERFOIN _____

f. GAGUE _____

g. GUENOT _____

h. ERUBAU _____

i. GUNOY _____

j. TRANELU _____

k. SARGENTE _____

PROOFREAD

If the sentence is correct, write *OK*. If a word is misspelled, cross it out and write it correctly on the line. The first one has been done for you.

a. I'm ~~ankshus~~ about my test results. _____*anxious*_____

b. It's none of your bussiness. _____

c. What a lovely bokay of flowers. _____

d. Try to maneuver your arm into the right position. _____

e. He speaks with a foreing accent. _____

f. She is a curteous salesclerk. _____

g. FBI stands for the Federal Burau of Investigation. _____

h. Empty gasolene cans were found in the burned-out building. _____

i. I'm completely against that idea. _____

j. You've got a beutiful voice. _____

k. He was promoted to the rank of sargent. _____

l. I have a souvineer of every city I've visited. _____

Answers start on page 125.

Spelling Errors Related to Pronunciation

WORDS TO KNOW

*athlete	*hundred	*pronunciation	*strictly
*attempt	*jewelry	*pursue	*submit
*because	*length	*quantity	*suggest
*besides	*library	*recognize	*supposed
*between	*mischievous	*representative	*surprised
*environment	*miniature	*respect	*tired
*equipment	*nuclear	*restaurant	*twelfth
*escape	*peculiar	*sandwich	*used to
*government	*probably	*secretary	*vehicle
*grievous		*strength	

As you know, we don't always write words the way we say them. In this section, we'll work on words that are often misspelled because of the way people say them in rapid speech.

When they come walkin in the door, he's gonna be so surprise!

In the sentence above, there are three spelling errors. The writer has put down the words exactly as she pronounces them, but her pronunciation has led to misspellings. Correctly spelled, the sentence would read:

When they come *walking* in the door, he's *going to* be so *surprised!*

Say the sentence out loud now, pronouncing the underlined words slowly. If you *pronounce* the words carefully and correctly, you'll also *spell* them correctly.

ING Ending

People often say "walkin'," "talkin'," "dancin'," and so on. This can cause them to forget to *write* the g of the **ing** ending. To remember the g in words like *walking, talking,* and *dancing,* be sure to pronounce the "ING" sound as you say the words. Also, keep in mind that **ing,** not -*in*, is a common verb ending.

Rule: Add *ing,* not -*in,* to verbs.

NOTE: Two common **ing** nouns are *morning* and *evening.*

PROOFREAD

Find and correct the twelve errors in *ing* words. The first one has been done for you.

walking
As I was ~~walkin~~ out of my house this mornin, I saw the mail carrier comin up the street pushin her cart. As she passed my neighbors' house, their dog came runnin out, barkin his head off. He jumped over the fence, ran up to the mail carrier, and began growlin and snappin at her. The mail carrier kept goin down the street, but I could see she was pullin a can of Mace out of her pocket. She didn't have to use it, though, because the dog stopped chasin her as soon as he saw she wasn't scared. The mail carrier said to me, "That's been happenin too much lately." I said, "Don't worry—all I've got is a canary, and it doesn't bite!"

Going to, Want to, Have Got to

I'm gonna leave now because I gotta take the bus and I don't wanna be late.

Because of his pronunciation, this writer has made several spelling mistakes. We often **say** "gonna," "gotta," and "wanna," but these are not words we should **write.** Here are the correct, complete spellings:

"gonna" ⟶ going to
"gotta" ⟶ (have or has) got to
"wanna" ⟶ want to

To remember these spellings, say these and other sentences *slowly* and *carefully:*

I'm *going to* leave now.
I've *got to* take the bus.
I don't *want to* be late.

Rule: Write *going to, (have/has) got to,* and *want to,* not *gonna, gotta,* or *wanna.*

PRACTICE

In your notebook, copy and complete these sentences.

a. Tomorrow I am going to. . . .

b. This week I've got to. . . .

c. In the future I want to. . . .

ED Adjectives

He was so surprise!

Can you see the spelling mistake? The word should be *surprised,* not *surprise.* In this sentence, *surprised* is an adjective that comes from a verb. Many adjectives use the **ed** verb form—the past participle. (Your instructor can tell you more about past participles and their use.) Here are some other examples of these **ed** adjectives. Say each sentence out loud, being sure to pronounce the **ed** ending. Here, the ending sounds like "D":

(surprise)   I am *surprised.*   (tire)   I am *tired.*   (worry)   I am *worried.*

Sometimes the **ed** ending sounds like "T." Say these sentences, pronouncing the **ed** as "T":

(bless)   She is *blessed.*
(suppose)   She is *supposed* to be here now.
(prejudice)   She is *prejudiced.*

If you pronounce these words carefully, you'll remember to write the **ed.**

―――――――――――――――――――― PRACTICE ――――――――――――――――――――

Complete each sentence with the correct **ed** adjective or verb. Add **ed** to the word in parentheses.

a. She is _____ to be a good singer.   (suppose)

b. I feel so _____.   (tire)

c. We _____ to play ball in an empty lot.   (use)

d. The boss is _____ against women.   (prejudice)

e. The store is _____ now.   (close)

f. I am _____ at your behavior.   (shock)

g. My hair is all _____ up.   (mess)

h. He had a _____ look on his face.   (surprise)

Final Consonant Sounds

I have a lot of respec for him.

Do you see the spelling error? The word is *respect,* not *respec.* When we speak, we don't always pronounce the final consonant clearly, and this can make us forget to write it. The solution is to be sure to pronounce clearly the last sound in words you want to learn to spell. In fact, it's helpful to exaggerate this final sound to keep it in your mind.

Final T ――――――――

Say each word below out loud and exaggerate the final *t.* Then circle the *t* and do the Say-Copy-Check exercise.

*attempt _____   *respect _____

 fact _____   *restaurant _____

 first _____   strict _____

 last _____   *suggest _____

49

What happens when we add *ly* to *strict*? We get *strictly*. It's hard to hear the *t* in this word, but remember to write it! Circle the *t* and do the Say-Copy-Check exercise.

*strictly _____

Final K

Say each word out loud, exaggerating the final *k*. Then circle the *k* and do the Say-Copy-Check exercise.

ask _____   risk _____

desk _____   task _____

Be sure to pronounce *ask* correctly; do not say "as' " or "ax." What happens when we add *ed* to *ask*? That's easy: ask + **ed** = _____ Be sure to write *asked*, not *ast* or *axed*.

Final D

Say each word out loud, exaggerating the final *d*. Then circle the *d* and do the Say-Copy-Check exercise.

band _____   hand _____

ground _____   understand _____

These final *t, k,* and *d* words are only a few examples. There are many more you'll need to know. Just remember: when you see a word whose spelling you want to learn, **exaggerate the pronunciation,** and you'll remember to write the last letter.

PROOFREAD

Find and correct the eleven errors in the passage below. The first one has been done for you.

respect
I have a lot of ~~respec~~ for my neighbor, Kiet, from Viet Nam. He has just opened a restauran that serves food from his country. This is his firs attemp at a business, and I hope it's not too big a ris. He works very hard, though, and the food is delicious. Also, Kiet stricly follows health regulations in food preparation.

Kiet and his wife work twelve hours a day at the restauran. Their children give them a han on the weekends, but Kiet hasn't axed them to give up their studies—he thinks education is too important. I wish Kiet the bes of luck, and I sugges that you try the food at his place soon.

Letter Reversal

The doctor wrote me a perscription.

The error in this sentence may be hard to find. The word is *PREscription*, not *PERscription*. If you mispronounce words by reversing their letters, you'll have the same trouble writing the letters in the correct order.

When you are trying to learn to pronounce and spell a word correctly, it often helps to break the word into syllables as you study it. If we break down *prescription,* we get:

pre scrip tion

The beginning clearly stands out as *pre,* not *per.*

Say each word below correctly. Look carefully at the order of the letters. Then copy each word once.

en vi ron ment	*environment	_____
hun dred	*hundred	_____
jew el ry	*jewelry	_____
nu cle ar	*nuclear	_____
per spire	perspire	_____
pre scrip tion	prescription	_____
pur sue	*pursue	_____
sec re tar y	*secretary	_____

Can you write a spelling trick for *secretary?* (Hint: Use the word *secret.*)

_____

PRACTICE

Fill in the missing words. Use the clues in parentheses.

a. It was so hot that he began to _____. (p—spire)

b. Let's look in the window of this _____ store. (j—ry)

c. She has her own _____. (se—tary)

d. He won a _____ dollars in the lottery. (hun—d)

e. Here's a _____ for a new pain killer. (p—scription)

f. Do you think _____ energy is safe? (nuc—ar)

g. He grew up in a loving _____. (env—ment)

h. She has lots of time to _____ her interests. (p—sue)

Letter Omission

The goverment was overthrown.

There is a common error in the sentence above. The word should be *government,* with an *n.* When we speak fast, we don't always pronounce each letter clearly, and, as a result, we may forget to write all of them. The solution is to pronounce words slowly and precisely when you are trying to learn to spell them.

Say each of the following words out loud, exaggerating the letters in bold type so you'll remember them. Circle these letters and copy the word once.

*gover**n**ment _____   *representative _____

*le**ng**th _____   *san**d**wich _____

*lib**r**ary _____   *stre**ng**th _____

*mi**n**iature _____   *su**b**mit _____

*pec**u**liar _____   *twel**f**th _____

*qua**n**tity _____   *ve**h**icle _____

*reco**g**nize _____

Here are some spelling tricks. Fill in the missing letters and then copy the tricks into your notebook.

Does the *GOVERNor GOVERN* the *GOVERNment?*

Does the _____ or _____ the _____ ment?

A *loNG leNGth* and a *stroNG streNGth.*

A lo____ le____th and a stro____ stre____th.

Some *SAND* got into my *SANDwich!*

Some _____ got into my _____ wich!

This *libRARy* has *RARe* books.

This lib____y has ____e books.

It's a *peCULiar CULt.*

It's a pe____iar ____t.

Her *MINIskirt* was *MINIature.*

Her _____skirt was _____ature.

PROOFREAD

If the sentence is correct, write *OK*. If a word is misspelled, cross it out and write it correctly on the line.

a. I don't have the strength to get up. _____

b. She collects miniature furniture. _____

c. Who is the leader of that goverment? _____

d. I almost didn't reconize you with that toupee! _____

e. Let's study in the libary. _____

f. What is the lenth of that sailboat? _____

g. He is our state represenative. _____

h. She lives on the twelfth floor. _____

i. They bought a large quanity of photo supplies. _____

j. Would you like a ham sanwich? _____

k. I will not submit to your evil wishes! _____

l. It was a most pecuiar situation. _____

m. This motor veicle is unregistered. _____

Syllable Omission

He's probly angry at me.

What's the mistake here? It should be *proBABly,* not *probly.* People sometimes leave out an entire syllable when they say a word, and, as a result, they forget to write it. Be sure to say every syllable in a word as you are learning to spell it.

Say each of the words below out loud. Then copy it once on the line.

be cause	*because _____
be sides	*besides _____
be tween	*between _____
prob a bly	*probably _____

Here is a spelling trick to help you remember all the letters in *probably*. Fill in the missing letters and then copy it into your notebook:

The *BABy* is *proBABly* sick.

The _____y is pro_____ly sick.

Write a sentence with each word:

(because) _____

(besides) _____

(between) _____

(probably) _____

Extra Letters and Syllables

She helped him ecscape.

What's wrong now? The writer has added an extra letter! The word is *escape*, not *eCscape*. Correct pronunciation will help you avoid these errors.

Correctly pronounce each word below and then copy it on the line.

ath lete	*athlete	_____
e quip ment	*equipment	_____
es cape	*escape	_____
griev ous	*grievous	_____
mis chiev ous	*mischievous	_____
pro nun ci a tion	*pronunciation	_____

PROOFREAD ———

Find and correct the six errors in the paragraph below.

Harry committed a grievious crime: he stole the team mascot. Now, Harry was a mischievious young man who loved to play practical jokes. One day, while all the other atheletes were on the field, Harry snuck into the locker room. He searched through all the equiptment until he found Gladys the goose—a toy that was the mascot of the Flapping Geese football team. With Gladys in a sack slung across his shoulder, Harry made his ecscape. No one noticed Gladys's absence until Harry innocently announced that he had received a ransom note, which he read aloud with exaggerated pronounciation: "Give me the goods, or Gladys gets it!" The team was on to Harry and didn't buy the kidnapping story. They stormed Harry's locker and found Gladys under a pile of dirty sweatshirts.

Answers start on page 125.

Review of Silent Vowels and Pronunciation Spelling Errors

As you do the next exercises, keep in mind all you've learned about words misspelled because of silent vowels or because of their pronunciation. If the sentence is correct, write *OK*. If a word is misspelled, cross it out and write it correctly on the line.

a. He's a born athelete. _____

b. Don't attempt to wake him up. _____

c. The gentleman was very courteous to the hostess. _____

d. I like you cuz you're nice. _____

e. Heavy industry has polluted our enviornment. _____

f. You need special equipment to play that game. _____

g. The sargeant ordered the recruit out of the barrack. _____

h. I work for the federal goverment. _____

i. She likes costume jewlery. _____

j. The nuclear family consists of a father, a mother, and children. _____

k. Her life story is a profile in curage. _____

l. You're probly wondering why I called you here. _____

m. Switzerland is a politically neutral country. _____

n. Her pronunciation is excellent. _____

o. Don't you reconize me? _____

p. He left his comb and brush on the bureau. _____

q. I'd like a tuna salad sanwich. _____

r. The secretary types fifty words per minute. _____

s. He doesn't know his own strenth. _____

t. The seatbelt law was not strickly enforced. _____

u. What am I suppose to do? _____

v. My daughter is very ankshus about her prom. _____

w. He crashed into the fence when he tried to maneuver the car out of the driveway. _____

Answers start on page 125.

Reduced Vowel Roots 1: A

WORDS
TO
KNOW

*academic	*magazine	*senator
*explanation	*permanent	*separate
*lavatory	*representative	*signature

custady?   custedy?   custidy?   custody?   custudy?

Of these five spellings, only one is correct: *custody,* with an *o.* How do you know? After all, we don't say "cust-OH-dy." In fact, the *o* sounds like "UH." At times, all of the other vowel letters sound like "UH" also. You can hear "UH" for the boldface vowel letter in each of the following words:

A—m**a**gazine   E—el**e**vator   I—acc**i**dent   O—cust**o**dy   U—vol**u**nteer

The "UH" sound in these words is called a **reduced vowel sound** because you don't hear a clear long or short vowel. This reduced vowel occurs in a syllable that is not stressed. Since the reduced vowel sound can be represented by any vowel letter, you can't tell by merely listening to the word whether it is spelled *custady, custedy, custidy, custody,* or *custudy.* You need to learn which words use which letters for the reduced vowel sound. In this chapter, we'll study the most important and trickiest words of this type.

All of these words have a reduced vowel represented by *a.* Circle the *a* that sounds like "UH" and do the Say-Copy-Check exercise. Capitalize the *a* the first time.

*ac(a)demic *ac**A**demic   academic*   *permanent _____

*explanation _____   *representative _____

*extraordinary _____   *senator _____

*lavatory _____   *separate _____

*magazine _____   *signature _____

Here are some spelling tricks. Fill in the missing letters and copy the tricks into your notebook:

That's *A sepARATE RATE.*

That's ____ sep____ ____.

She got an *A* for her *acAdemic* work.

She got an ____ for her ac____demic work.

GAZe at the maGAZine.

_____e at the ma_____ine.

Try writing some of your own spelling tricks. Use the hints in parentheses.

senator (Hint: Use *at*.) _____

explanation (Hint: Use *an*.) _____

And remember: *extraordinary* is simply *extra* + *ordinary*.

PROOFREAD ————

If the sentence is correct, write *OK*. If a word is misspelled, cross it out and spell it correctly on the line.

a. Her acodemic progress has been good. _____

b. Where is the employees' lavatory? _____

c. What an extrordinary idea! _____

d. There's got to be a logical explination. _____

e. He was reading a magizine. _____

f. There was no permanent damage. _____

g. She's our state representitive. _____

h. He's our senitor. _____

i. They have seperate bank accounts. _____

j. Your signature is illegible. _____

Answers start on page 125.

Reduced Vowel Roots 2: E

WORDS TO KNOW	*benefit	*counselor	*maintenance	*vegetable
	*bulletin	*elevator	*repetition	
	*category	*enemy	*specific	
	*cemetery	*irrelevant	*tragedy	

All of these words have the "reduced E." Circle the *e* and do the Say-Copy-Check exercise, capitalizing the *e* the first time.

*benefit _____   *irrelevant _____

*bulletin _____   *maintenance _____

*category _____   *repetition _____

*cemetery _____   *specific _____

*counselor _____   *tragedy _____

*elevator _____   *vegetable _____

*enemy _____

Here are some spelling tricks. Fill in the missing letters and copy the tricks into your notebook.

LET me see the *bulLETin.*

_____ me see the bul_____in.

The *mainTENance* costs *TEN* dollars.

The main_____ance costs _____ dollars.

GET me the *veGETable* knife.

_____ me the ve_____able knife.

Captain *NEMo* is my *eNEMy.*

Captain _____o is my e_____y.

Can you write spelling tricks for these words? Use the hints in parentheses.

cemetery (Hint: Use *met.*) _____
tragedy (Hint: Use *GED.*) _____

PROOFREAD —————

If the sentence is correct, write *OK*. If a word is misspelled, cross it out and write it correctly on the line.

a. This bullatin board is full of papers. _____

b. Our building has a new maintanence man. _____

c. That's an irrelevant question. _____

d. It was a terrible tragidy. _____

e. Have some vegtable soup. _____

f. We went to the cematery last week. _____

g. You can't put her in any special category. _____

h. What benifits do you receive? _____

i. Take the elavator to the twenty-first floor. _____

j. The career counselor gave me good advice. _____

k. They crashed in enamy territory. _____

l. This endless repatition is boring. _____

m. Please be spacific. _____

Answers start on page 126.

Reduced Vowel Roots 3: ER

WORDS
TO
KNOW

*average	*general	*literature
*conference	*governor	*preference
*desperate	*interest	*temperature

Watch out for *er* in the middle of a word. Sometimes the *e* is reduced so much that you hardly hear it. But even though a word like *interest* may sound like "intrest," remember to write that *e!* When you pronounce the word exactly the way it should be written, it will be easier to spell.

Circle *er* and do Say-Copy-Check, capitalizing the *er* the first time. When doing the Say-Copy-Check exercises, pronounce each word as it is written so that you remember to write the "reduced ER" sound.

*average _____   *interest _____

*conference _____   *literature _____

*desperate _____   *preference _____

*general _____   *temperature _____

*governor _____

PRACTICE

Fill in the missing "reduced ER" word.

a. He didn't express any _____—he doesn't care which movie we choose.

b. My savings account earns 7 percent _____.

c. My boss is attending a national _____ in Washington, D.C.

d. The _____ outside is eighty degrees.

e. The _____ of our state is a Republican.

f. He has a good batting _____.

g. She likes to read, so she plans to study _____.

h. In _____, we don't eat a lot of sweets. Once in a while, though, I permit myself a donut.

i. After he lost his job, Mitch was _____ for money.

Answers start on page 126.

Reduced Vowel Roots 4: I

WORDS TO KNOW

*accident	*definite	*holiday	*president
*alibi	*eligible	*hospital	*privilege
*candidate	*engineer	*medicine	*repetitive
*cigar	*evident	*optimistic	*responsibility
*coincidence	*fascinate	*original	*significant

The following words have the "reduced I." Circle the reduced *i* and do the Say-Copy-Check exercise, capitalizing the *i* the first time.

*accident _____   *definite _____

*alibi _____   *eligible _____

*candidate _____   *engineer _____

*cigar _____   *evident _____

*coincidence _____   *fascinate _____

Here are some spelling tricks. Fill in the missing letters and copy the tricks into your notebook.

DID our *canDIDate* win?   *FINd* a *deFINite* answer.

_____ our can_____ate win?   _____d a de_____ite answer.

═══════════════════ PRACTICE ═══════════════════

Fill in the missing "reduced I" word.

a. The movie didn't _____ me, but it was fairly interesting.

b. I lost it by _____.

c. You grew up in Philadelphia? So did I. What a _____!

d. He lit up a big, fat _____.

e. He's the Democratic _____ for president.

f. You say you didn't commit the crime that night. What's your

_____?

g. What do you mean you're not coming? I thought our plans were

_____.

h. He wants to be an electrical _____.

i. Which _____ bachelor will you pick?

j. We hold these truths to be self-_____.

Here are some more words with the "reduced I." Circle the reduced *i* and do the Say-Copy-Check exercise, capitalizing the reduced *i* the first time.

*holiday _____   *president _____

*hospital _____   *privilege _____

*medicine _____   *repetitive _____

*optimistic _____   *responsibility _____

*original _____   *significant _____

PROOFREAD ————

If the sentence is correct, write *OK*. If a word is misspelled, cross it out and write it correctly on the line.

a. The lesson was very repetative. _____

b. Try to be optamistic. _____

c. Some day, a woman will be president. _____

d. Voting is a right, not a privelege. _____

e. It's not my responsability. _____

f. There's a significant difference between the two findings.

_____

g. Take your medecine. _____

h. Tomorrow's a holyday. _____

i. He's in the hospital. _____

j. What an origanal idea! _____

Answers start on page 126.

Reduced Vowel Roots 5: O

WORDS TO KNOW	*apologize	*gasoline	*laundromat
	*chocolate	*hypocrite	*opinion
	*custody	*innocent	*opposite
	*customer		

These words all have the "reduced O." Circle the "reduced O" and do the Say-Copy-Check exercise, capitalizing the *o* the first time.

*apologize _____   *hypocrite _____

*chocolate _____   *innocent _____

*custody _____   *laundromat _____

*customer _____   *opinion _____

*gasoline _____   *opposite _____

To remember the "reduced O" in these words, you can exaggerate your pronunciation as you study them. Say "apol-OH-gize," "cust-OH-mer," and so forth. (Of course, this is not the normal pronunciation to use in regular speech. Use it just to help you learn the spelling.)

PRACTICE

Fill in the missing "reduced O" words.

a. He's not guilty; he's _____.

b. He washed his clothes at the _____.

c. What's your _____ on the president's South African policy?

d. After the divorce, the mother retained _____ of the children.

e. I'd like to _____ for the terrible things I've done.

f. Don't drop a lighted match in this pool of _____.

g. The _____ is always right. That's our store policy.

h. You actually *liked* that movie? I had the _____ reaction.

i. He criticizes me for my diet, and then I see him eating hot dogs and French fries. What a _____!

j. I love _____ sundaes.

Answers start on page 126.

Reduced Vowel Roots 6: OR

WORDS TO KNOW	*favorite	*ignorant	*laboratory	*opportunity

Say each word out loud and exaggerate the pronunciation of *or*. Then circle the *or* and do the Say-Copy-Check exercise, capitalizing the *or* the first time.

*favorite _____

*ignorant _____

*laboratory _____

*opportunity _____

PROOFREAD ——————

If the sentence is correct, write *OK*. If a word is misspelled, cross it out and write it correctly on the line.

a. He's my favrite TV star. _____

b. Don't act so ignorant! _____

c. She works in a labratory. _____

d. He took every oppertunity to walk all over me. _____

Answers start on page 126.

Reduced Vowel Roots 7: U

WORDS TO KNOW	*luxury	*prejudice	*Saturday	*volunteer

These words have the "reduced U." Circle the "reduced U" and do the Say-Copy-Check exercise, capitalizing the *u* the first time.

*luxury _____   *Saturday _____

*prejudice _____   *volunteer _____

Here are some spelling tricks. Fill in the missing letters and copy the tricks into your notebook.

It's your *TURn* on *SaTURday*.

It's your _____n on Sa_____day.

It's *pURe luxURy*.

It's p_____e lux_____y.

─────────────────── PRACTICE ───────────────────

Fill in the missing "reduced U" words.

a. We must fight against _____ and hatred.

b. _____ and Sunday are my favorite days.

c. You can obtain good experience by doing _____ work.

d. Her goal is to live in the lap of _____.

OTHER REDUCED VOWELS ───────

SPECIAL NOTE: The following words all contain different reduced vowels. Learn them. Circle the underlined reduced letter(s) in each word and do the Say-Copy-Check exercise.

*analysis _____

*bicycle _____

*mischievous _____

*restaurant _____

Now keep in mind all the words you have just studied.

PROOFREAD ——————

Find and correct the sixteen misspelled words in the passage below. The first one has been done for you.

general

In ~~general~~, when it comes to ideal living quarters, most people have a defanite prefrence. Some people would like to live in a luxery high-rise. In a high-rise, you never have to climb stairs because there is an elavator. You never have to haul your clothes to the laundrymat because there's a laundry room in the building. Many buildings also have seperate storage rooms, bicicle rooms, and party rooms. Some even have their own restarants. And since the building has a full-time maintinance staff, you never have to worry about hiring a plumber, carpenter, or painter.

Other people would rather have their own home in the suburbs. Even though you must take full responsability for the upkeep of the house, you have many benifits. You have more privacy, and you can play your favrite music as loud as you want without disturbing your neighbors. You have your own big yard to relax in—if you don't mind spending Saterday mowing the lawn! And you may feel that a real house seems more perminent than an apartment.

Of course, most of us don't have the privelege of choosing the ideal living situation, but we can always dream.

Answers start on page 126.

Reduced Vowel Suffixes 1: ENT/ENCE and ANT/ANCE

WORDS TO KNOW

*absence	*coincidence	*experience	*nuisance	*presence
*acquaintance	*confidence	*guidance	*obedience	*reference
*apparent	*convenient	*ignorant	*performance	*significant
*assistant	*dependent	*instance	*permanent	*superintendent
*attendance	*descendant	*insurance	*pleasant	*tenant
*audience	*evident	*irrelevant	*preference	*vengeance
*balance	*existence	*maintenance		

In this section, you'll work on word endings that sound alike or are otherwise tricky. These words contain reduced vowel suffixes, or reduced suffix endings that begin with vowel letters.

ENT/ENCE and ANT/ANCE Endings

Your attendance(?) has been good. You have only one absance(?)
attendence(?)   absence(?)

There is no automatic way to know that the words should be spelled *attendance* and *absence*. This is because the reduced vowel sound can be represented by any vowel letter. There are two ways to deal with this problem: learn which endings are used in certain common words and use your dictionary any time you are not sure.

Here are some words that end in *ent* or *ence*. Say each out loud, exaggerating the pronunciation of the ending to help you remember it. Circle the ending and do the Say-Copy-Check exercise, capitalizing the ending the first time.

*appar(ent)   *apparENT*   *apparent* _____   *experience _____

*audience _____   *preference _____

*coincidence _____   *president _____

*confidence _____   *reference _____

*existence _____   *superintendent _____

Here are some spelling tricks. Fill in the missing letters and copy the tricks into your notebook.

PARENTs' duties are *apPARENT*.

_____ s' duties are ap_____.

The *coinciDENce* was *coinciDENtal*.

The coinci_____ce was coinci_____tal.

The following words have *ant* or *ance*. Say each word out loud, exaggerating the pronunciation of the ending to help you remember it. Circle the ending and do the Say-Copy-Check exercise, capitalizing the ending the first time.

*acquaintance _____   *nuisance _____

*balance _____   *performance _____

*descendant _____   *pleasant _____

*guidance _____   *tenant _____

*insurance _____   *vengeance _____

*maintenance _____

Here is a spelling trick to help you remember that *descendant* ends in *ant*. Fill in the missing letters and copy the trick into your notebook.

You act like the *descendANT* of an *ANT*.

You act like the descend_____ of an _____.

Can you write spelling tricks to remember the *ant* and *ance* in the next words? Use the hints in parentheses.

acquaintance (Hint: Use *dance*.) _____

balance (Hint: Use *lance*.) _____

insurance (Hint: Use *chance*.) _____

performance (Hint: Use *trance*.) _____

tenant (Hint: Use *ant*.) _____

PROOFREAD 1 ———

Keep in mind the *ent*/*ence* and *ant*/*ance* words you have studied. Cross out the misspelled word and write it correctly on the line.

a. audiance   performance   insurance   _____

b. pleasant   apparant   descendant   _____

c. coincidence   maintenence   conference   _____

d. apparent   superintendent   tenent   _____

e. preferance   insurance   nuisance   _____

f. experience   conference   guidence   _____

Word Pairs

conveni*ent*   conveni*ence*

These two words can be called a **word pair** because of their similar endings. *Convenient* ends in *ent* (not *ant*) and *convenience* ends in *ence* (not *ance*). If you know the spelling of one word in the pair, you'll also know the spelling of the other.

There are several *ent*/*ence* word pairs. In each pair, if one word ends in *ent*, the other will end in *ence* and vice versa. Play around with some of these.

Circle the *ent* in the words below. Copy the word and then write the correct *ence* form.

*conven(ent)   *convenient   convenience*

*dependent _____

*evident _____

*permanent _____

Now circle the *ence*. Copy the word and then write the correct *ent* form.

*absence _____

*confidence _____

*obedience _____

*presence _____

There are also word pairs with *ant/ance*. Circle the *ant* or *ance* ending in each of the following words. Then copy the word and write the corresponding *ant* or *ance* form.

*assistant _____

*attendance _____

*ignorant _____

*instance _____

*irrelevant _____

*significant _____

It is helpful to learn these word pairs because, if you know the spelling of one word, you automatically know that of the other word.

PROOFREAD 2 ———

Cross out the misspelled word in the pairs below and write it correctly on the line.

a. sign~~ificence~~ significant   *significance* _____

b. absence   absant _____

c. evidance   evident _____

d. instant   instence _____

e. dependant   dependence _____

f. assistent   assistance _____

g. permanent   permanance _____

h. ignorence   ignorant _____

i. presance   present _____

j. obedient   obediance _____

Answers start on page 126.

Reduced Vowel Suffixes 2: OR and AR

WORDS TO KNOW

*ancestor	*familiar	*professor
*author	*governor	*radiator
*burglar	*grammar	*senator
*calculator	*honor	*similar
*calendar	*humor	*spectator
*conductor	*odor	*sponsor
*counselor	*particular	*supervisor
*dollar	*peculiar	*survivor
*elevator	*popular	*visitor

auth*or*   burgl*ar*

In the words above, the endings sound alike but are spelled differently. Let's study words with each ending.

OR Ending

A number of words end in *or*. Say each word out loud, exaggerating the pronunciation of the *or* ending to help you remember the spelling. Then circle *or* and do the Say-Copy-Check exercise.

*ancestor _____

*author _____

*calculator _____

*conductor _____

*counselor _____

*elevator _____

*governor _____

*honor _____

*humor _____

*odor _____

Fill in the missing *or* words you have just studied.

a. Who is the _____ of this book?

b. The _____ of the garbage dump made me hold my nose.

c. The _____ said, "All aboard!"

d. Take the _____ to the tenth floor.

e. The _____ has decided to run for a second term.

f. We are going to _____ our boss at a big banquet.

g. You should discuss your problems with a _____.

h. I don't believe that Mary is descended from George Washington. She once told me that Abraham Lincoln was also her _____.

i. I can't add or subtract anything without my pocket _____.

j. She has a great sense of _____.

Here are some more *or* words. Say each word out loud, exaggerating the pronunciation of the *or* ending. Circle the *or* and do the Say-Copy-Check exercise.

*professor _____   *sponsor _____

*radiator _____   *supervisor _____

*senator _____   *survivor _____

*spectator _____   *visitor _____

Fill in the missing *or* words you've just studied.

a. Richard is a _____ of physics at the university.

b. The _____ didn't keep all his campaign promises.

c. There was only one _____ of the shipwreck.

d. I'm sorry. The hospital allows only one _____ at a time. Come back again tomorrow during visiting hours.

e. It's too cold in here. Turn on the _____.

f. And now, a word from our _____.

g. At work, my _____ watches me like a hawk.

h. Do you like _____ sports, or do you prefer to participate in them?

AR Ending

Only a few words end in *ar*. Say each word below out loud, exaggerating the *ar* ending. Then circle the *ar* in each word and do the Say-Copy-Check exercise.

*burglar _____   *particular _____

*calendar _____   *peculiar _____

*dollar _____   *popular _____

*familiar _____   *similar _____

*grammar _____

════════════════════ PRACTICE 3 ════════════════════

Fill in the correct word with the *ar* ending. The first one has been done for you.

a. Do you like _____*popular*_____ music?

b. Don't I know you? Your face looks _____.

c. It only costs one _____.

d. He wandered around. He had no _____ place to go.

e. Mark the date on your _____.

f. They make a _____-looking couple: he's seven feet tall, and she's only four feet, five inches.

g. Your apartment isn't exactly like mine, but it's _____.

h. A _____ broke into our house while we were out of town.

i. Be sure to use good _____ in your English composition.

PROOFREAD ——————

Keep in mind everything you've learned about words with the *or* and *ar* endings. Cross out the misspelled word and write it correctly on the line.

a. teacher   writer   auther   _____

b. robber   burgler   mugger   _____

c. buyer   dancer   visiter   _____

d. doller   customer   peculiar   _____

e. calender   register   trailer   _____

f. designer   worker   spectater   _____

g. hammer   discover   oder   _____

Answers start on page 126.

72

Reduced Vowel Suffixes 3: ABLE/IBLE

WORDS TO KNOW	*available	*eligible	*indispensable	*possible	*reversible	*susceptible
	*convertible	*flexible	*inevitable	*reliable	*sensible	*terrible
	*desirable	*horrible	*legible	*responsible	*suitable	*visible

ABLE/IBLE Endings

terr*ible?*   terr*able?*   return*ible?*   return*able?*

How do you know when to add *able* or *ible?* This time, there is a general rule to guide you. You can learn it by working through these examples. The correct words above are *terrible* and *returnable*. Now take the endings off these words. What's left?

terr   return

Of the two, which one is the word that can stand alone? (Circle one.)

terr   return

Which ending do you add to *return?* (Circle one) *able ible*
Which ending do you add to *terr?* (Circle one) *able ible*

Rule: We usually add *able* to words that can stand alone: return + *able* = *returnable*. We usually add *ible* to roots that cannot stand alone: terr + *ible* = *terrible*.

PRACTICE

Fill in the words with the correct *able* or *ible* ending according to the rule. (Remember to drop the *e* before adding these suffixes and change *y* to *i*.)

a. return _____   i. adore _____

b. terr _____   j. desire _____

c. horr _____   k. poss _____

d. wash _____   l. incred _____

e. accept _____   m. profit _____

f. elig _____   n. suscept _____

g. rely _____   o. suit _____

h. vis _____   p. avail _____

(Is *avail* a word? Check your dictionary!)

Of course, there are some exceptions to the rule. These *ible* words come from words that can stand alone. Circle the *ible* and do the Say-Copy-Check exercise.

*convertible _____

*flexible _____

*responsible _____

*reversible _____

*sensible _____

The *able* words below come from roots that cannot stand alone. Circle *able* and do the Say-Copy-Check exercise.

indispensable _____

*inevitable _____

PROOFREAD

If the sentences below are correct, write *OK*. If a word is misspelled, cross it out and write it correctly on the line.

a. You've made a horrable mistake. _____

b. The bike rider was barely visable in the dark. _____

c. In this movie, Sophia Loren plays a desirible older woman. _____

d. Would it be possible for us to change seats? _____

e. It was inevitible that the children would leave home. _____

f. Try to act like a responsable adult. _____

g. Bernie is a reliable employee. _____

h. A good manager must be firm yet flexable. _____

i. The Millers did not think Cliff was a suitible husband for their daughter. _____

j. This jacket is reversable. _____

k. Your help has been indispensible. _____

Answers start on page 126.

Reduced Vowel Suffixes 4: LE/EL/AL

WORDS TO KNOW	*article	*muscle	*official	*proposal	*symbol
	*capital	*neutral	*physical	*quarrel	*travel
	*hospital	*nickel	*practical	*rival	*vehicle
	*model	*occasional			

pickle?   pickel?   pickal?

The endings *le, el,* and *al* all sound alike. How do you know when to use each?

LE Ending

Le is the most common ending. Here are just a few examples: *ample, ankle, beetle, bottle, circle, double, handle, pickle, settle, thimble,* and *triple.* Can you think of any more?

Make sure also that you know these three *le* words. Circle the *le* and do the Say-Copy-Check exercise.

*article _____   *muscle _____   *vehicle _____

━━━━━━━━━━━━━━ PRACTICE 1 ━━━━━━━━━━━━━━

Fill in the missing *le* word on the line, using the letters in parentheses as a guide.

a. Draw a _____ around the right answer.   (cir—)

b. Buy a _____ of ketchup.   (bott—)

c. He read a newspaper _____ about cancer.   (artic—)

d. You're in big _____, mister!   (troub—)

e. Feel my arm _____.   (musc—)

f. Do not drive a car or any motor _____ on this path.
   (vehic—)

AL Ending

The *al* ending is commonly used on adjectives. In the words below, circle the *al* and do the Say-Copy-Check exercise.

*neutral _____

*occasional _____

*official _____

*physical _____

*practical _____

Some nouns also use *al*. In the words below, circle the *al* and do the Say-Copy-Check exercise.

*capital _____   *proposal _____

*hospital _____   *rival _____

━━━━━━━━━━━━━━━━━━━ **PRACTICE 2** ━━━━━━━━━━━━━━━━━━━

Fill in the correct *al* words.

a. It's OK to have an _____ beer, but don't overindulge.

b. She is a _____ education teacher, and she believes that daily exercise is important.

c. This jacket is a _____ color, so you can wear it with anything.

d. Aunt Lillian stayed in the _____ for one week after her surgery.

e. Another word for competitor is _____.

f. The committee submitted a _____ to the board of directors.

g. These shoes are not very elegant, but they are _____.

h. What is the _____ seal of the Department of Justice?

EL Ending

El is used less frequently than *le* or *al*. Make sure you know these four words. Circle the *el* and do the Say-Copy-Check exercise.

*model _____   *quarrel _____

*nickel _____   *travel _____

NOTE: *nickel* may also be spelled *nickle,* but this spelling is less common.
Can you write some spelling tricks to recall the *el* in the words? Write one trick for each *el* word. (Hint: Use the name *Ellen* or the word *elevator*.)

(model) _____

(quarrel) _____

(travel) _____

One common word ends in *ol*. Circle the *ol* and do the Say-Copy-Check exercise.

*symbol _____

You can hear the *o* better in a different form of the word. Remember: *symbol—symbolic.*

PROOFREAD

If the sentence is correct, write *OK*. If a word is misspelled, cross it out and write it correctly on the line.

a. We need to make a practicle decision. _____

b. In generel, we write *i* before *e* except after *c*. _____

c. They quarrel all the time. _____

d. They went to the hospitle. _____

e. Read this magazine artical. _____

f. Don't mention the rivel brand in the ad. _____

g. Flex your muscle! _____

h. She's a top fashion modal. _____

i. In some paintings, the lily is a symbol of purity. _____

Answers start on page 126.

Reduced Vowel Suffixes 5: ARY/ERY/ORY

WORDS TO KNOW	*boundary	*grocery	*memory	*secretary
	*cemetery	*history	*necessary	*summary
	*dictionary	*machinery	*ordinary	*victory

ARY Ending

boundary?   boundery?   boundory?

Ary is a much more common ending than *ery* or *ory*. Circle *ary* and do the Say-Copy-Check exercise.

*boundary _____   *ordinary _____

*dictionary _____   *secretary _____

*necessary _____   *summary _____

────────── PRACTICE 1 ──────────

Fill in the missing *ary* word.

a. Look the word up in the _____.

b. Is it _____ to pay sales tax on food in this state?

c. This fence marks the _____ between your property and mine.

d. Don't get dressed up. Just wear _____ everyday clothes.

e. Write a _____ of the story.

f. My _____ will set up an appointment with you.

ERY Ending

Four common words end in *ery*. Circle the *ery* and do the Say-Copy-Check exercise.

*cemetery _____   *machinery _____

*grocery _____   *stationery _____

The word *stationery* here means writing paper. Here is a spelling trick to help you remember the *e* in *ery*. Fill in the missing letters and copy the trick into your notebook.

StationERY is *lettER papER*.

Station_____ is lett____ pap____.

Fill in the missing *ery* words.

a. Pick up some apples at the _____ store.

b. The plant manufactures heavy _____.

c. John F. Kennedy is buried at Arlington National _____.

d. Miss LaRue writes letters on perfumed _____.

ORY Ending

Three common words end in *ory*. Circle the *ory* and do the Say-Copy-Check exercise.

*history _____

*memory _____

*victory _____

You can remember the *o* if you think of other forms of these words in which it's easier to hear it: *history—historical, memory—memorial, victory—victorious.*

PROOFREAD

If the sentence is correct, write *OK*. If a word is misspelled, cross it out and write it correctly on the line.

a. Give me a summery of the situation. _____

b. Do you like to study histery? _____

c. The dictionary is a speller's best friend. _____

d. The club secretery read the minutes of the last meeting. _____

e. It's not necessery to eat an apple every day. _____

f. Victory is ours! _____

g. They're still working with the machinary. _____

h. She has personalized stationary. _____

i. Someone vandalized the cemetery. _____

j. Amnesia is the loss of memery. _____

Answers start on page 126.

Reduced Vowel Suffixes 6: AIN/ON/OM

WORDS TO KNOW	*bargain	*common	*opinion	*poison	*wagon
	*certain	*mountain	*pardon	*villain	*wisdom

AIN Ending

This dress is a real   barg**ain.** (?)
                     barg**on.** (?)

The right spelling is *bargain*. The **ain** ending sounds like "IN" and occurs in several words. Circle the **ain** and do the Say-Copy-Check exercise.

*bargain _____

*certain _____

*mountain _____

*villain _____

PRACTICE 1

Fill in the missing **ain** words.

a. Climb the _____.

b. This radio is only fifteen dollars. What a _____!

c. The _____ stole money from old Mrs. Lacey.

d. I'm not absolutely _____ about the answer.

ON/OM Ending

A number of words ending in **on** or **om** also sound like "IN" or "IM." Circle the **on/om** and do the Say-Copy-Check exercise.

*common _____

*opinion _____

*pardon _____

*poison _____

*wagon _____

*wisdom _____

PRACTICE 2

Fill in the missing **on/om** words.

a. They have absolutely nothing in _____.

b. _____ me? I didn't hear you.

c. Their car is a station _____.

d. What's your _____ on this matter?

e. He acquired all his _____ through many years of study.

f. He tried to _____ himself with cyanide.

Answers start on page 126.

Reduced Vowel Suffixes 7: ACY/ASY

WORDS TO KNOW	*democracy	*ecstasy	*fantasy	*hypocrisy	*privacy

ecstacy?   ecstasy?   privacy?   privasy?

To find out which spellings are correct, work through the exercises below.

ACY Ending

Two common words end in *acy*. Circle the *acy* and do the Say-Copy-Check exercise.

*democracy _____   *privacy _____

ASY Ending

Two common words end in *asy*. Circle the *asy* and do the Say-Copy-Check exercise.

*ecstasy _____   *fantasy _____

Here is a spelling trick to help you remember the *as* in both words: Fill in the missing letters and copy the trick into your notebook.

His *fanTAStic fanTASy* left him in *ecsTASy*.

His fan_____tic fan_____y left him in ecs_____y.

One word ends in *isy*. Circle the *isy* and do the Say-Copy-Check exercise.

*hypocrisy _____

Here is a spelling trick to help you remember this ending. Copy the trick in your notebook.

CRIStina does not believe in *hypoCRISy*.

PROOFREAD ——————

If the sentence is correct, write *OK*. If a word is misspelled, cross it out and write it correctly on the line.

a. Her fantacy is to travel around the world. _____

b. How many nations practice true democracy? _____

c. Hypocracy disgusts me. _____

d. Mmmmm. This chocolate cream pie has me in ecstacy. _____

e. I can't get privasy even in my own home! _____

Answers start on page 126.

Reduced Vowel Suffixes 8: Tricky Endings

**WORDS
TO
KNOW**

*crisis	*develop	*purchase
*criticism	*furnace	*salad
*damage	*private	*standard

Other Words with Tricky Endings

There are several other words whose endings are commonly misspelled. Circle the boldface ending in each word and do the Say-Copy-Check exercise. Be sure to capitalize the ending the first time you copy the word.

*cris**is** _____   *stand**ard** _____

*critic**ism** _____   *furn**ace** _____

*dam**age** _____   *prejud**ice** _____

*devel**op** _____   *priv**ate** _____

*sal**ad** _____   *purch**ase** _____

Here are some spelling tricks to help you remember the spellings of these endings. Fill in the missing letters and copy the tricks into your notebook.

POP will *develOP* the pictures.

P____ will devel____ the pictures.

This *salAD* tastes *bAD!*

This sal____ tastes b____!

RACE down to the *furnACE.*

R_____ down to the furn_____.

That's a *standARD cARD* trick.

That's a stand_____ c_____ trick.

PrejudICE isn't *nICE.*

Prejud_____ isn't n_____.

PROOFREAD 1 ————

If the sentence is correct, write *OK*. If a word is misspelled, cross it out and write it correctly on the line.

a. I'd like to purchace a camera. _____

b. It was a standard-size hotel room. _____

c. I'll have soup and saled. _____

d. We need to develope our plans for the future. _____

e. She can't take any criticism. _____

f. The furness exploded. _____

g. Prejudus is an ugly thing. _____

h. She had a private room. _____

i. He is experiencing an identity crises. _____

j. Was there much damige on your car? _____

You've studied words with difficult endings. You will undoubtedly encounter new words with tricky endings. Remember: to learn tricky endings, exaggerate the pronunciation as you study the word. If you are not sure of the ending to a word, you should always consult your dictionary! Now test the knowledge you have gained.

PROOFREAD 2 ————

Find and correct the twelve errors in this passage.

The tenent upstairs is rather strange. Because he's always afraid a burgler will break into his house, he decided to purchis bars for his door. That in itself is not strange, but these bars are permanant—they don't open, so he has to climb through the window. Once inside, he puts rat poisin on the window ledge, although I don't know why he thinks that will deter anyone from entering.

I was shocked when he actually went away on a three-day vacation. During his absance, he left on a tape recording that continuously played the sound of a dog barking. He didn't ask me or my neighbors to look after his place. He is certinly not a friendly man. He has tacked up a marked calender and a piece of personal stationary that says: "Visiters: Please sign up in advance. I'm only availible on the indicated days. I value my privasy." I'll bet you no one has ever signed up!

Answers start on page 127.

Getting Lost in Long Words

The **Delacration** of **Inpedence** was signed in 1776.

This sentence was taken from a student's history paper. It's obvious what the writer meant to say, but look carefully at the two boldface words. Are they spelled correctly? No! Although it seems as if the writer had *some* idea of what letters went into each word, he wasn't sure of the order and just slapped them down any which way.

Errors like this look careless and silly. They are easy to make—especially when you're writing quickly—but they are equally easy to correct. If you tend to "get lost in words," the solution is to proofread carefully what you've written, sounding out the long words. For example, look back at the phrase "Delacration of Inpedence." Let's sound out the first attempt:

"Delacration"—del a cra tion

Is that a word? No! The correct word is pronounced "dec la ra tion": *declaration*. Write the correct spelling on the line below, saying the word syllable by syllable as you write:

_____

Now sound out the second attempt:

"Inpedence"—in pe dence

That's not a word! It should be pronounced "in de pen dence": *independence*. Copy the word below, saying it correctly syllable by syllable:

_____

Always check your spelling by sounding out the word syllable by syllable.

=================== PRACTICE ===================

Correct the misspelled words in the following sentences. Sound out your corrections as you write them.

a. The Delacration of Independence was signed in 1776. _____

b. His face looked famliar. _____

c. What is the denifition of this word? _____

d. She has an avdantage over me. _____

e. This is a facsintating book. _____

f. Please try to be more speficic. _____

g. The tempterature was too high. _____

h. He was a superior althete. _____

i. He is my mortal emeny. _____

Answers start on page 127.

Past Tense and Past Participles

1. a. Did he *buy* something?
   b. Yes, he *bought* another tie.
   c. He has *bought* three ties this week.

2. a. Did she *drive* today?
   b. Yes, she *drove* to work.
   c. She has *driven* to work every day this week.

In the questions above, we see the **base forms** of two verbs: *buy* and *drive*. The base form is what you start with when you form any verb tense. In sentences 1b and 2b, we see the **past forms** of these verbs: *bought* and *drove*. In sentences 1c and 2c, we see the **past participles** of the verbs: *bought* and *driven*.

Past participles are used with the helping words—has, have and had.

Examples: The dog *has* *bitten* the postman.   He *had* *fallen* from the ladder.
I *have* *completed* the assignment.

Some verbs, like *buy*, have the same past form and past participle: *buy—bought—bought*. Other verbs, like *drive*, have different past forms and past participles: *drive—drove—driven*. In any case, both the past forms and past participles are used frequently, so spelling errors in these words stand out.

Here is a list of commonly misspelled past forms and past participles. Say each out loud and do the Say-Copy-Check exercise. The first time capitalize the letters in bold type.

Verbs with the Same Past Forms and Past Participles

Base Form	Past Form/Past Participle		
read	read	*rEAd*	*read*
lead	led		
keep	kept		
sleep	slept		
sweep	swept		
feel	felt		
mean	meant		
bend	bent		
build	built		
lend	lent		
send	sent		
spend	spent		
cost	cost		
find	found		
hold	held		
say	said		

Base Form	Past Form
bring	brought _____
buy	bought _____
fight	fought _____
think	thought _____
catch	caught _____
teach	taught _____
sell	sold _____
tell	told _____
sit	sat _____
lose	lost _____
shoot	shot _____
dig	dug _____
hang	hung _____
lay	laid _____
pay	paid _____
strike	struck _____
win	won _____

Verbs with Different Past Forms and Past Participles

Base Form	Past Form	Past Participle
drive	drove *drOve* *drove*	driven *dr9ven* *driven*
ride	rode _____	ridden _____
write	wrote _____	written _____
break	broke _____	broken _____
choose	chose _____	chosen _____
freeze	froze _____	frozen _____
speak	spoke _____	spoken _____
steal	stole _____	stolen _____
wake	woke _____	woken _____
swear	swore _____	sworn _____
tear	tore _____	torn _____
wear	wore _____	worn _____
blow	blew _____	blown _____
fly	flew _____	flown _____
grow	grew _____	grown _____

Base Form	Past Form	Past Participle
know	knew _____	known _____
throw	threw _____	thrown _____
draw	drew _____	drawn _____
eat	ate _____	eaten _____
give	gave _____	given _____
fall	fell _____	fallen _____
shake	shook _____	shaken _____
take	took _____	taken _____
begin	began _____	begun _____
drink	drank _____	drunk _____
run	ran _____	run _____
sing	sang _____	sung _____
swim	swam _____	swum _____
forget	forgot _____	forgotten _____
get	got _____	gotten _____
bite	bit _____	bitten _____
hide	hid _____	hidden _____
be	was/were _____	been _____
see	saw _____	seen _____
lie	lay _____	lain _____

PRACTICE 1

Answer each question using the correct *past* form. Use your notebook.

Example: When did you last *sweep* the floor?

I swept it yesterday.

a. What magazines did you *read* last week?

b. How many hours did you *sleep* last night?

c. How did you *feel* yesterday?

d. When did you *leave* the house this morning?

e. How much did your TV *cost?*

f. How much money did you *spend* at the supermarket last week?

g. What did you *buy* at the supermarket?

h. What movie did you last *see?*

i. What did you *think* of that movie?

j. What did you *tell* your friends about the movie?

k. When did you last *write* a letter?

l. When did you last *speak* to a doctor?

m. When did you last *take* a bus?

n. What did you *drink* with your dinner last night?

o. When did you *begin* to work on your spelling?

p. When did you last *forget* something? (What was it?)

q. When did you *pay* your last phone bill?

―――――――――― **PRACTICE 2** ――――――――――

Fill in the correct *past* participle.

a. He has _____ many hurtful things. (say)

b. They have _____ many innocent people to their graves. (lead)

c. She has _____ sick all morning. (feel)

d. Our instructor has _____ us a lot about spelling. (teach)

e. They have _____ bravely for their honor. (fight)

f. How many reports have you _____? (write)

g. Have you ever _____ a motorcycle? (ride)

h. She has _____ a new set of dishes. (choose)

i. They've _____ everything! (steal)

j. They have _____ the truth for years now. (know)

k. Have you _____ lunch yet? (eat)

l. He has _____ in love again. (fall)

m. They've just _____ fired. (get)

n. Where have you _____ my glasses? (hide)

o. He's _____ in Nevada for three years. (be)

Past participles are often used as adjectives. Fill in the correct past participle/adjective.

a. Remove the _____ nail from the wall.   (bend)

b. I'm sorry. This car is _____.   (sell)

c. My nerves are really _____!   (shoot)

d. It's a _____ cause.   (lose)

e. I demand a _____ apology.   (write)

f. This chair is _____.   (break)

g. Buy some _____ vegetables when you're at the store. (freeze)

h. These are _____ goods.   (steal)

i. My shoes are all _____ out.   (wear)

j. Their clothes were ripped and _____.   (tear)

k. He gave a _____ statement.   (swear)

l. She was badly _____ by the accident.   (shake)

m. You are _____.   (drink)

Answers start on page 127.

Finding Difficult Past Forms and Past Participles

He *broke* (?) *brocke* (?) the window.   The window is *broken* (?) *brocken* (?).

If you don't know the spelling of a past form or a past participle, what can you do? By now, you should be quite familiar with the answer: use the dictionary. But what exactly will you look up? Think of the base form of the word and find that. You'll see the past form and past participle listed there if they are irregular or difficult.

The base form of the word above is *break.* If you look it up, you'll find something like this:

break (brāk) *v.* broke, broken, breaking ----------------

Before the **ing** form, you see the past form, *broke,* and the past participle, *broken.*

Remember that some words have the same past form and past participle. If you look up a word like *shoot,* you'd find this entry:

shoot (sho͞ot) *v.* shot, shooting ----------------

In this case, *shot* is both the past form *and* the past participle.

PRACTICE

Look at the misspelled past forms and past participles in the sentences below. Look up the base form of the words in the dictionary and then fill in the correctly spelled base form, past form, and past participle. The first one has been done for you.

	Base	**Past**	**Participle**
a. He *brock* his leg. The dish is *brocken.*	*break*	*broke*	*broken*
b. He *knowed* the answer. He has *knowen* it a long time.			
c. He *lead* her astray. He has *lead* a bad life.			
d. She *feeled* good. She has *fell* good all day.			
e. She *drunk* some wine. She has *drunken* all of it.			
f. She *tolled* a lie. She has *tol* lots of lies.			

Answers start on page 127.

You have studied words with silent vowels, spelling errors related to pronunciation, words with reduced vowels, and past forms and past participles. Test your knowledge now.

Review Test

Using the clues in parentheses, fill in the missing words. You will need to add one or more letters to the clue.

a. The _____ was elected by a majority vote. (represen—tive)

b. Look at the notices on the _____ board. (bul—in)

c. She has _____ you three letters, and you haven't responded. (wri—en)

d. The space shuttle flight ended in _____. (tra—dy)

e. The _____ was a pleasant seventy-two degrees. (temp—ure)

f. The father was granted _____ of the children. (cus—dy)

g. We can wash all of our clothes at the _____ down the street. (laund—mat)

h. The biology class will meet in the _____ this afternoon. (lab—tory)

i. I've _____ you a gift. (bro—t)

j. My nephew is a _____ fire fighter. (vol—teer)

k. It soon became _____ that she was going to be awarded the party nomination. (appar—t)

l. The sheriff hunted the cowboy with a _____. (veng—ce)

m. The former _____ of schools is a woman. (superintend—t)

n. I'll circle the date on my _____ so I won't forget it. (cal—r)

o. There were only five _____ from the airplane crash. (survi—rs)

p. This snake wrench comes in handy. It is really _____. (indispens—)

q. I need a driver's license in order to drive this _____. (vehi—)

r. He bought an _____ rubber gasket and inserted it inside the hose. (ordin—y)

s. He _____ he loved her more than anyone else. (sa—)

t. The old witch put a deadly _____ in his soup. (pois—)

u. What can compare to the _____ of a first love? (ecs—y)

v. My husband and I want to _____ some new appliances. (purch—)

Answers start on page 127.

SECTION 3

Confusing Words

   Words that Sound Alike

   Words that Sound Almost Alike

   Words that Look Almost Alike

Words to Use

   Contractions and Possessives

Words for Now

   A Letter of Complaint

Dictionary Exercise

   Finding Confusing Words

CONFUSING WORDS

Words that Sound Alike

allowed   aloud

a. Smoking is not _____ in the classroom.

b. Do you read _____ to your children?

The words *allowed* and *aloud* have the same pronunciation. Do you know which belongs in Sentence a and which in Sentence b? (If not, you'll find out shortly.)

In English, there are a number of words that have the same pronunciation but are spelled differently. We'll work on some of these troublemakers in this section.

Read each definition and look at the correct spelling. The first word listed is the more common one. Do the Say-Copy-Check exercise, capitalizing the letters in bold type the first time. Then do the fill-in-the-blank exercise. Finally, write a sentence with each word in your notebook.

1. **ALLOWED—ALOUD**

(past of allow; permitted) all**owed** _____

(out loud) al**oud** _____

a. Say your name _____.

b. She _____ her children to stay up late last night.

c. Smoking is not _____ here.

2. **ALTER—ALTAR**

(to change) al**ter** _____

(part of a house of worship) alt**ar** _____

a. We had to _____ our plans.

b. The priest left the _____.

c. The tailor will _____ my new suit.

3. **BASE—BASS**

(foundation or bottom) ba**se** _____

(musical instrument) ba**ss** _____

a. Andrew plays the _____ in our band.

b. The _____ of the wall is pure concrete.

c. At the _____ of all his problems was an unhappy childhood.

4. BIRTH—BERTH

(being born) birth _____

(bed on ship or train) berth _____

a. Ralph was thrilled at the _____ of his first child.

b. The sailor rolled off his _____.

c. The scientist gave _____ to a new theory.

5. BREAK—BRAKE

(damage or destroy) break _____

(stopping device) brake _____

a. Step on the _____ pedal.

b. If you _____ a mirror, you'll have seven years of bad luck.

c. Don't _____ your promise to me.

6. CAPITAL—CAPITOL

(government city; money or property; most important or prominent; punishable by death)
capital _____

(main *building* of the government) capitol _____

Here is a spelling trick. Fill in the missing letters and copy the trick into your notebook.

The *capitOl* has a *gOld dOme*.

The capit__l has a g__ld d__me.

a. Ottawa is the _____ of Canada.

b. The reconstruction of the _____ building is almost done.

c. What's your opinion of _____ punishment?

d. Use a _____ letter at the beginning of a sentence.

e. To open a business, you need _____.

7. CEREAL—SERIAL

(breakfast food) cereal _____

(a series, one after another) serial _____

Here's a spelling trick. Fill in the letters and write the trick in your notebook:

A *SERIal SERIes*. A _____al _____es.

a. The _____ murderer was finally arrested.

b. I don't like oatmeal or any other hot _____.

c. There's a new _____ on TV.

8. COLONEL—KERNEL

(a position in the military) **colo**nel _____

(a grain) **ker**nel _____

a. He got a _____ of corn stuck in his teeth.

b. There's a _____ of truth in that statement.

c. He was promoted to the rank of _____.

9. COMPLIMENT/COMPLEMENT/COMPLIMENTARY/COMPLEMENTARY

(praise) compliment _____

(go along with or balance out) complement _____

a. These shoes _____ your outfit perfectly.

b. I'd like to _____ you on your excellent work.

c. He gave her a _____.

(full of praise, free of charge) complimentary _____

(going along with or balancing out) complementary _____

d. She received many _____ glances when she got her new hairdo.

e. The business partners had _____ skills; Mr. Lee was good with numbers, and Mr. Park was good with people.

f. All passengers will receive a _____ beverage.

10. CORD—CHORD

(rope or twine) **c**ord _____

(musical blending of sound) **ch**ord _____

a. Tie up the package with strong _____.

b. Can you play that _____ on your guitar?

c. If you keep yelling, you'll damage your vocal _____s.

(NOTE: This part of the anatomy is stringlike.)

11. COUNSEL—COUNCIL/COUNSELOR—COUNCILLOR

(verb: to advise; noun: advice) coun**sel** _____

(governing or advisory group or commission) coun**cil** _____

a. The minister will give you good _____.

b. The city _____ will meet to vote on the bond issue.

c. Psychologists _____ people with emotional problems.

(someone who counsels or advises) coun**selor** _____

(a member of a council) coun**cillor** _____

(NOTE: This word is rare.)

d. The career _____ suggested that I study business.

12. FAIR—FARE

(just or equal; a festival) **fair** _____

(transportation fee) **fare** _____

a. Is it _____ for men to get paid more than women?

b. What is the plane _____ from here to Los Angeles?

c. There will be a street _____ here next weekend.

13. FOURTH—FORTH

(4th) **fourth** _____

(forward) **forth** _____

Here are some spelling tricks. Fill in the missing letters and copy the tricks into your notebook.

FOUR in _FOURth._   _____ in _____th

FORward is _FORth._   _____ward is _____th.

a. That's the _____ time he's called this morning!

b. Only one-_____ of the voters came out for that election.

c. He walked back and _____ .

14. HEAL—HEEL

(make better, cure) **heal** _____

(part of a foot or shoe) **heel** _____

a. Don't walk long distances until your blisters _____ .

b. The shoe repair man put a new _____ on my left shoe.

c. They shook hands and decided to _____ their friendship.

15. HEAR—HERE

(listen) **hear** _____

(not there) **here** _____

Here are two spelling tricks. Fill in the missing letters and copy the tricks into your notebook.

HEAR with your _EAR._   _____ with your _____.

HERE and _tHERE._   _____ and t_____

a. What? I can't _____ you!

b. I'm over _____ .

c. She doesn't _____ a thing you say.

16. HORSE—HOARSE

(an animal) horse _____

(husky sound) hoarse _____

a. Have you ever ridden a _____?

b. The police put up saw _____s to block off the street.

c. He got _____ from yelling so much.

17. HOLE—WHOLE

(dug-out space or gap) hole _____

(complete) whole _____

a. There's a _____ in the wall.

b. He ate the _____ thing.

c. It's a _____ new idea.

18. ISLE—AISLE

(island) isle _____

(space between rows) aisle _____

a. What would you take with you to a desert _____?

b. I always like to sit in an _____ seat in the theater.

c. The bride walked down the _____.

19. LEAD—LED

The word *lead* has two pronunciations. As a verb in the present tense it rhymes with *seed*. (**Example:** Don't *lead* me on.) As a noun it rhymes with *bed*. (**Example:** *lead* poisoning)

(noun: a metallic element) lead _____

(past form of the verb *lead*) led _____

a. He _____ the horses to a stream.

b. It's dangerous for children to eat paint with _____ in it.

c. You _____ me to believe that you were faithful, but I just saw you with another woman!

20. LESSON—LESSEN

(a study unit; something you learn) lesson _____

(to make less) lessen _____

a. If you stop smoking now, you can _____ the damage to your lungs.

b. In this _____, you'll study words that sound alike.

c. I really learned my _____ from that experience.

21. MEET—MEAT

(encounter; get together) meet _____

(animal flesh) meat _____

a. I'll _____ you at noon.

b. I'm pleased to _____ you.

c. I like to eat _____ and potatoes.

22. MINOR—MINER

(small; not important; under age eighteen) minor _____

(a mine worker) miner _____

You can hear the *o* better in another form of the word. Just remember *minor—minority*.

a. The coal _____ got trapped in the mine.

b. You are a _____, so we cannot serve you alcohol.

c. We're happy with this car. It has given us only _____ problems.

23. NAVAL—NAVEL

(related to the navy) naval _____

(belly button) navel _____

a. She's a _____ officer.

b. The bikini revealed her _____.

c. The ships conducted _____ maneuvers off the coast.

24. PASSED—PAST

(past tense of *pass;* went by) passed _____

(opposite of present or future) past _____

a. In the _____, people rode horses instead of driving cars.

b. Can't we stop now? We've already _____ three restaurants.

c. He _____ up a golden opportunity.

25. POLE—POLL

(rod or stick) pole _____

(questionnaire or survey) poll _____

a. He bought a new fishing _____.

b. The newspaper conducted a _____ to predict the election outcome.

c. I wouldn't touch him with a ten-foot _____.

26. POUR—PORE

(to flow or make flow) pour _____

(a tiny opening in the skin; to examine carefully) pore _____

a. Use this makeup to minimize your _____s.

b. Could you _____ me some lemonade?

c. I have to _____ over this instruction manual.

27. PRINCIPAL—PRINCIPLE

(main or major; school director) princip**al** _____

(basic truth or law; ethical standard) princip**le** _____

a. She lives by a strict set of moral _____s.

b. Their _____ export is rice.

c. Johnny was sent to the office of the _____.

28. PROFIT—PROPHET

(money left after expenses; benefit from) pro**fit** _____

(someone who predicts the future correctly) pro**phet** _____

a. The oil company made a huge _____ last year.

b. You can _____ from mistakes if you learn from them.

c. In the Muslim religion, Moses, Jesus, and Mohammed are considered _____s.

29. ROLL—ROLE

(type of bread; twirl around; list of names) ro**ll** _____

(a part you play) ro**le** _____

a. _____ over and go to sleep.

b. The teacher called the _____.

c. What _____ did Clint Eastwood play in *Pale Rider?*

d. I'd like a _____ with my salad.

30. STAKE—STEAK

(a large peg; something to lose or gain) st**ake** _____

(kind of meat) st**eak** _____

a. I like my _____ medium rare.

b. The tree was supported by a wire attached to a _____ in the ground.

c. We all have a _____ in the success of this deal.

31. STATIONERY—STATIONARY

(writing paper) station**ery** _____

(still, not moving) station**ary** _____

Here are some spelling tricks. Fill in the missing letters and copy the tricks into your notebook.

StationERy is *lettER papER.*   Station___y is lett___ pap___.

StAnd stationAry.   St___nd station___ry.

a. Good _____ is expensive.

b. The tank was _____ for hours; then it finally began to move.

c. In the card store, they sell all kinds of _____.

98

32. TOO—TO—TWO

(also; excessive) **too** _____

(toward; part of a verb) **to** _____

(2) **two** _____

a. Go _____ the store.

b. I have _____ brothers.

c. You are _____ noisy. Please be quiet.

d. I have a Toyota, and my sister has one, _____.

e. I like _____ swim.

33. VAIN—VEIN

(proud; useless) **vain** _____

(blood vessel) **vein** _____

a. She is a _____ woman.

b. She has a large blue _____ in her forehead.

c. He tried in _____ to revive the old man.

34. WASTE—WAIST

(verb: use badly; noun: garbage) **waste** _____

(middle part of the body) **waist** _____

a. Don't _____ your time or your money.

b. She has a twenty-inch _____.

c. This is a toxic _____ dump.

PROOFREAD ———

Keep in mind all of the sound-alike words you've studied as you do this exercise. If the sentence is correct, write *OK*. If a word is misspelled, cross it out and write it correctly on the line.

a. Don't altar your plans for me. _____

b. She gave berth to a beautiful baby boy. _____

c. Be careful not to brake your leg. _____

d. Madison is the capital of Wisconsin. _____

e. Ann Landers often advises people to seek counciling. _____

f. You cheated! That's not a fare move. _____

g. Please come here. _____

h. That's a hole new idea. _____

i. He led me up the garden path. _____

j. He plays for the miner leagues. _____

k. He past up a perfectly good opportunity. _____

Answers start on page 127.

Contractions and Possessives

Look at the following lists of words:

LIST A		**LIST B**	
who's	you're	whose	your
it's	they're	its	their

All of the words in List A are *contractions*. Write the complete form of each:

who's = _____*who is*_____   you're = _____

it's = _____   they're = _____

PRACTICE 1

In your notebook, *copy* each sentence and then *rewrite* it using a contraction.

a. *Who is* going to help me?

Who is going to help me?   *Who's going to help me?*

b. *It is* my favorite show.   d. He says that *you are* a good cook.

c. I don't know what *they are* doing.   e. I have a friend *who is* seven feet tall.

Now look back to List B. All of these words are *possessives*. That is, they tell us about possession or ownership. Remember that possessive pronouns do *not* take the apostrophe.

PRACTICE 2

Write the correct possessive: *whose, its, your,* or *their.*

a. _____ book is this? It isn't mine.

b. Please help me. I need some of _____ good advice.

c. They invited me to _____ house for dinner.

d. I have a friend _____ father is a lawyer.

e. The nation honored _____ heroes.

It's easy to confuse contractions and possessives when you are writing quickly, but if you stop and think for just a minute, it's also easy to write the correct form. Try these examples:

WHO's or *WHOSE?*

1. _____ briefcase is this?   2. _____ knocking on the door?

We know that *who's* is a contraction of *who is*. Can we say "*Who is* briefcase is this?" ? No! That's nonsense. Therefore, we can't write *who's* in Sentence 1. Can we say "*Who is* knocking on the door?" ? Of course! Therefore, we know we can write *who's* (*who is*) in Sentence 2.

Returning to Sentence 1, how do we know for sure that we should write *whose*? First remember that *whose* is a possessive. Is Sentence 1 asking about possession, or ownership? Yes. The person wants to find the *owner* of the briefcase. So it's clear that we can write *whose* in Sentence 1: "Whose briefcase is this?"

Any time you are uncertain whether or not to write a *contraction* (*who's, it's, you're,* or *they're*), break the word down into its complete form (*who is, it is, you are,* or *they are*). If the complete form fits logically into the sentence, you can use the contraction. If not, you probably need a *possessive* (*whose, its, your,* or *their*). You can double check by asking yourself if the sentence is talking about possession or ownership.

Try the following exercises, keeping in mind the above hints.

—————————— PRACTICE 3 ——————————

Fill in *who's* or *whose*.

a. _____ dancing with Clarence?

b. _____ car are you going to use?

c. Look at the man _____ playing that tuba.

d. There's the man _____ wife won the lottery.

—————————— PRACTICE 4 ——————————

Fill in *it's* or *its*.

a. _____ a gorgeous day.

b. The cat ate _____ dinner.

c. Is the water ready? Yes, _____ boiling.

d. The building is so old that _____ stairs are falling down.

—————————— PRACTICE 5 ——————————

Write *you're* or *your* in the correct space. The first one has been done for you.

a. Take _____ grubby hands off me!

b. _____ doing an excellent job.

c. I can't hear what _____ saying.

d. Leave all _____ troubles behind.

—————————— PRACTICE 6 ——————————

Write *they're* or *their* in the correct space.

a. I know where _____ hiding.

b. _____ wonderful people.

c. _____ son is charming.

d. I like _____ apartment.

Now watch out because there's another word that sounds like *they're* and *their*—it's the word *there*. *There* is used to show location: "Look over *there!*" Just remember: *here and there*. *There* is also used in the phrases *there is* and *there are*:

> *There is* a good band playing at Ernie's.

> *There are* many reasons why I like this city.

Now keep in mind:

> THEY'RE—a contraction of *they are*

> THEIR—related to possession

> THERE—used for location or in the phrases *there is* and *there are*

———————————————— PRACTICE 7 ————————————————

Write *they're, their,* or *there* in the correct space.

a. Don't go in _____.

b. _____ just asking for trouble.

c. _____ children are all grown up.

d. _____ is a great Mexican restaurant near my house.

Study the review chart:

CONTRACTIONS	POSSESSIVES	OTHER
who's (who is)	whose	
it's (it is)	its	
you're (you are)	your	
they're (they are)	their	there (location; *there is/are*)

PROOFREAD

If the sentence is correct, write *OK*. If a word is misspelled, cross it out and write it correctly on the line. The first one has been done for you.

a. Who's going to take out the garbage? _____

b. Your going to love it! _____

c. Someone broke into the museum and stole it's most famous painting.

_____

d. There are three new students in our class. _____

e. Do you know who's notebook this is? _____

f. I went over to see they're new baby. _____

g. Do you have you're driver's license with you? _____

h. It's so nice to see you again. _____

i. I know a man whose going to have open heart surgery.

_____

j. Their living in a tiny apartment above a grocery store.

_____

k. It looks like its going to be another long day. _____

l. Their is no one at home. _____

Answers start on page 127.

Words that Sound Almost Alike

He took a pitcher (?) picture (?) of the house.

You have worked on words that sound alike but are spelled differently. In this section, you'll work on words that are often confused because they sound *almost* alike. The key here is to pronounce each word carefully so that you can hear the difference between the spellings.

In the exercise below, read each definition and say the word out loud. Be sure to pronounce the word slowly and carefully. (Pronunciation hints are given in parentheses.) Do the Say-Copy-Check exercise, capitalizing the letters in bold type. Then complete the fill-in-the-blank exercises that follow. Finally write a sentence with each word in your notebook.

1. **ACCEPT—EXCEPT**

   (to agree to; receive; approve; believe in) (Exaggerate the A and say "ACcept.") **acc**ept _____

   (not including) (Say "EXcept.") **ex**cept _____

   Here are some spelling tricks. Fill in the missing letters and copy the tricks into your notebook.

   Please *Accept* my *Apology*. Please __ccept my __pology.

   I like everyone *EXcept* my *EX-husband*.

   I like everyone ____cept my ____-husband.

   a. I _____ your invitation.

   b. They took everything _____ the kitchen sink.

   c. He can't _____ the fact that his wife is dead.

2. **ADDITION—EDITION**

   (something added) (Say "ADDition.") **add**ition _____

   (a version or issue of a book) (Say "EDition.") **ed**ition _____

   a. They spent a million dollars on the _____ to the hospital.

   b. Let's order the new _____ of the biology textbook.

   c. _____ and subtraction are two basic skills everyone should know.

3. **ADVICE—ADVISE**

   (a *noun* meaning suggestion) (The *c* has the "S" sound so the word rhymes with *nice*.)
   advice _____

   (a *verb* meaning to counsel or give advice) (The *s* has the "Z" sound, so the word rhymes with *wise*.) advise _____

   Here are two spelling tricks. Fill in the missing letters and copy the tricks into your notebook.
   NICE advICE.   N_____ adv_____

   Let a *wISE* man *advISE* you.   Let a w_____ man adv_____ you.

   a. I _____ you to see a doctor.

   b. Here's some _____ for you.

c. My _____ is to save your money carefully.

4. AFFECT—EFFECT

(a *verb* meaning to have an impact on) **affect** _____

(a *noun* meaning a result or consequence) (Say "EEEEffect.") **effect** _____

Study these examples:

This medicine will not *affect* your stomach.

This medicine will not have *an effect* on your stomach.

Now look at the spelling tricks. Fill in the missing letters and copy the tricks into your notebook.

That doesn't *AFFect* my *AFFection* for you.

That doesn't _____ect my _____ection for you.

My friend *EFFie* had a big *EFFect* on me.

My friend _____ie had a big _____ect on me.

a. Will the operation _____ her ability to walk?

b. The child's tantrum had no _____ on his parents.

c. This discovery could _____ the lives of thousands.

d. Did the movie _____ you, or did it leave you cold?

e. Will the new policy have an _____ on your job hours?

   NOTE: Occasionally, you will see the word *effect* used as a verb, as in the phrase "to effect change" meaning "to cause or bring about." Be careful! This usage is not common.

5. BURY—BERRY

Many people pronounce these words exactly alike. However, it may help you to pronounce them differently in order to learn their spellings.

(a *verb* meaning to put under the ground.) (Say "BURRRRy.") **bury** _____

(a *noun* meaning a small fruit.) (Say "BERry.") **berry** _____

a. Our dog died last week. We will _____ him in our backyard.

b. Don't eat that wild _____. It might be poisonous.

c. Let's _____ the past and think about the future.

6. CONSCIENCE—CONSCIOUS—CONSCIENTIOUS

(a *noun* meaning the part of you that tells you right from wrong) (Say "con-shense.")

conscience _____

(an *adjective* meaning awake or aware) (Say "con-shuss.") **conscious** _____

(an *adjective* meaning diligent or hardworking) (Say "con-shē-en-shuss.")

conscientious _____

a. My _____ told me not to do it.

b. Don't worry. He is _____. That blow didn't knock him out.

c. He is a _____ employee. He always works carefully.

7. DEVICE—DEVISE

(a *noun* meaning a thing or machine) (This word rhymes with *ice*.) device _____

(a *verb* meaning to make up or create something) (This word word rhymes with *disguise*.)
devise _____

Here are two spelling tricks. Fill in the missing letters and copy the tricks into your notebook.

An *ICE devICE*.   An _____ dev_____.

DevISE a *disguISE*.   Dev_____ a disgu_____.

a. This handy _____ will simplify your life.

b. We need to _____ a plan to escape.

c. A corkscrew is a _____ that opens wine bottles.

8. FORMALLY—FORMERLY

(officially; not casually; *formal* + ly) (Say "for-MA-lee.") formally _____

(in the past; not anymore; *former* + ly) (Exaggerate the *r*. Say "for-MER-ly.")
formerly _____

a. He was dressed _____.

b. _____, he was a policeman. Now, he's a lawyer.

c. You will be _____ introduced to the queen during your visit.

9. GUESS—GUEST

(*noun:* an estimate; *verb:* to make an estimate) guess _____

(a visitor) (Be sure you pronounce the *t* at the end.) guest _____

a. _____ what! I got a new job!

b. Please be my _____.

c. I didn't know for sure that he was at the tavern. It was just a _____.

10. ILLUSION—ALLUSION

(a vision that is not true) (Say "ILLusion.") illusion _____

(a reference) (Say "ALLusion.") allusion _____

a. This line of the poem is an _____ to something in the Bible.

b. Black clothes can create the _____ of slenderness.

c. It was just an _____; it wasn't real.

11. LIABLE—LIBEL

(likely to; responsible for) (Say "li-a-bull.") liable _____

(false accusation) (Say "li-bel.") libel _____

a. If you keep playing with that gun, you're _____ to hurt someone.

b. I hold you _____ for that accident.

c. When the reporter said she was a prostitute, Mrs. Lewis sued the station for _____.

12. LOSE—LOOSE

(a *verb* meaning to forget) (The *s* has a "Z" sound, and the word rhymes with *booze*.)

lose _____

(an *adjective* meaning not tight) (The *s* has the "S" sound, and the word rhymes with *noose*.)

loose _____

Here is a spelling trick. Fill in the missing letters and copy the trick into your notebook.

A *lOOse nOOse*.   A l____se n____se.

a. These pants are too _____.

b. Be careful not to _____ this important paper.

c. I win, and you _____.

13. METAL—MEDAL—MEDDLE

(a material such as steel) (Emphasize the *t*. Say "MET-al.") **met**al _____

(a small token or disk awarded as a prize) (Emphasize the *d*. Say "MED-al.")

medal _____

(to interfere) **med**dle _____

a. Gold is a precious _____.

b. He was awarded a _____ for his bravery.

c. There was a _____ bar across the door.

d. Don't _____ in the affairs of others.

14. PETAL—PEDAL—PEDDLE

(part of a flower) (Emphasize the *t*. Say "PET-al.") **pet**al _____

(*noun:* part of a car or bicycle; *verb:* to pump with your feet) (Emphasize the *d*. Say "PED-al.")

pedal _____

(to sell in the street) **ped**dle _____

a. You'll have to _____ fast to keep up with the other bikers.

b. Those men _____ watches and other stolen goods.

c. A rose _____ fell to the floor.

d. Something is wrong with the gas _____.

15. PICTURE—PITCHER

(*noun:* a painting or photo; *verb:* to imagine) (Say "pick-chur.") **pic**ture _____

(a water vessel; a ball thrower) (Say "pitch-er.") **pitch**er _____

a. This is a _____ of my Uncle Albert.

b. The _____ struck him out.

c. The nurse put a _____ of water near the patient's bed.

d. In my mind, I can _____ my dream home.

16. PRECEDE—PROCEED

(to happen first or before) (Say "PREEEEE-cede.") **prece**de _____

(to continue or go ahead) (Say "PRO-ceed.") **proc**eed _____

REMEMBER: *pre* means "before."

a. The easy lessons will _____ the hard ones. It's always best to start simply.

b. You may _____ with the investigation.

c. Richard will remain at the office, but the rest of us will _____ to the construction site.

17. WEATHER—WHETHER

Some people pronounce these words differently while others say them exactly alike. To learn the correct spelling, however, it may help you to differentiate them.

(related to the sun, wind, and other elements) **wea**ther _____

(if) (Say "HWether.") **whe**ther _____

a. Did you have good _____ on your trip?

b. I don't know _____ to laugh or cry.

c. I'll marry you _____ or not my parents approve.

Keeping in mind everything you have learned about words that sound almost alike, do the following exercise.

PROOFREAD ———————

If the sentence is correct, write *OK*. If a word is misspelled, cross it out and write it correctly on the line.

a. The edition of two rooms to the house will cost thousands of dollars. _____

b. Please except this gift as a token of my appreciation. _____

c. That's excellent advise, but it will be hard to follow. _____

d. She became conscious of a pain in her right toe. _____

e. A grater is a devise used to grate cheese. _____

f. The basement was formally used as a playroom, but now it's been converted to a study.

_____

g. We have a guess staying at our home. _____

h. If you want to loose weight, go on a diet. _____

i. To correct her back problem, she had to have a medal rod inserted in her spine.

_____

j. The proceeding program was brought to you by Health Nutt Granola Bars. _____

Answers start on page 128.

A Letter of Complaint

Have you ever sent for something you didn't receive? Have you ever gotten a bill that you had already paid? Have you ever been treated rudely by someone over the phone or in a store? If you've experienced these or similar problems, you might wish to write a letter of complaint to the proper authorities.

A list of useful words is presented below. Copy these words into your notebook.

USEFUL WORDS

Nouns	Verbs	Adjectives/Adverbs
attention	appreciate	cancelled
complaint	complain	damaged
credit	credit	defective
problem	enclose	impolite(ly)
*purchase	pay—paid	missing
refund	*purchase—purchased	previous(ly)
replacement	*receive	rude(ly)
	replace	
	resolve	

PROOFREAD

In the following letters of complaint, find and correct a total of eleven errors.

Dear Sir or Madam:

Yesterday I recieved a bill from your company for $25.99. I payed this bill last month and am inclosing a copy of the canselled check to prove it. Please creddit my account accordingly. Thank you for your atention.

Sincerely,
Louis Richardson
Louis Richardson

Dear Sir or Madam:

I ordered a set of cookware from you six months ago. It finally arrived yesterday, but it was diffective. Two of the pots were mising, and the frying pan was damiged. I am returning the set to you and would apreciate a complete reffund as soon as possible.

Yours truly,
Teresa Alvarez Ochoa
Teresa Alvarez Ochoa

Answers start on page 128. 109

Words that Look Almost Alike

They want to adapt (?) adopt (?) a child.

Do you know which word is correct? The words *adapt* and *adopt* look similar, but they are pronounced differently. Say them correctly: *adApt* has the "short A" sound, so the word rhymes with *wrapped*. *AdOpt* has the "short O" sound, so it rhymes with *popped*. Now do you know which word is right for the sentence? Check yourself: *adopt* is correct.

There are many sets of words like *adapt—adopt* that look almost alike but are pronounced differently. If you learn the correct pronunciation for each, you'll be able to spell them correctly.

In the exercises below, read the definition of each word. Say it out loud carefully, noting the pronunciation hints in parentheses. Do the Say-Copy-Check exercise and then fill in the blanks.

1. **ADAPT—ADOPT**

(to change or alter as necessary) (This word has "short A" to rhyme with *wrapped*. Say "APT—adAPT.") ad**apt** _____

(to take another's child legally as your own; to choose and follow) (This word has "short O," so it rhymes with *popped*. Say "OPT—adOPT.") ad**opt** _____

a. If you go to live in another country, you must _____ to many new situations.

b. The Weinbergs want to _____ a baby.

c. The old plan isn't working, so we must _____ an entirely different one.

2. **ALLEY—ALLY**

(small street behind buildings) (The *ey* sounds like a "long E." Say "al-lee.")
al**ley** _____

(a person or country that works for or fights with you) (The *y* sounds like a "long I." Say "al-lie.") al**ly** _____

a. France is an important _____ of the United States.

b. Don't walk through a dark _____ at night.

c. He's not my enemy; he's my _____.

3. **ALONE—ALONG**

(solitary; by yourself) (Say "a-lone.") al**one** _____

(in line with; with) (Say "a-long.") al**ong** _____

a. They walked _____ the river.

b. He was all _____ in the world.

c. Leave me _____!

4. **ANGEL—ANGLE**

(a heavenly being) (This word has the "soft G" sound [like "J"].) an**gel** _____

(the figure formed by two lines coming from one point; position) (This has the "hard G" sound, so it rhymes with *tangle*.) **angle** _____

Here are some tricks. Fill in the missing letters, then copy the tricks into your notebook.

An *anGELic anGEL*   An an_____ic an_____

Don't *tANGLE* with this *ANGLE*.   Don't t_____ with this _____.

a. The building forms a right _____ with the ground.

b. From this _____, you look very slim.

c. The _____ had white wings and a golden harp.

5. BREATH—BREATHE

(a *noun* meaning the intake of air) (Say "breth" to rhyme with *death*.)

breath _____

(a *verb* meaning to take a breath) (Say "breeeeeeethe" to rhyme with *seethe*.)

breathe _____

a. Help! I can't _____!   c. Don't _____ the poisonous fumes.

b. It's like a _____ of fresh air.

6. CLOSE—CLOTHES—CLOTH

(opposite of open) (This word rhymes with *nose*.) **close** _____

(dresses, shirts, slacks, etc.) (Be sure to pronounce the *th* in this word.)

clothes _____

(fabric) (This word rhymes with *moth*.) **cloth** _____

a. Please _____ the door.

b. She wears very fashionable _____.

c. Use a soft _____ to polish your car.

7. COMA—COMMA

(a state of deep unconsciousness) (This word has a "long O" sound.)

coma _____

(a punctuation mark) (This word has a "short O" sound.) **comma** _____

a. He was in a _____ following the accident.

b. A _____ is used for punctuation.

8. COSTUME—CUSTOM

(outfit or special clothes) (Say "cos-tyoom" or "cos-toom.")

costume _____

(a tradition; made to order) (Say "cuss-tum.") **custom** _____

a. It was his _____ to give his secretary candy every Friday.

b. He wore a _____-made suit.

c. On Halloween, Freddy wore a Superman _____.

111

9. DAIRY—DIARY

(related to milk products; a place where milk products are produced) (Say "dai-ry.")

dairy _____

(a book you write in every day) (Say "di-a-ry.") diary _____

a. She was mad when her younger brother read her _____.

b. Cheese and yogurt are _____ products.

c. He kept a _____ of his travels.

10. DECEASED—DISEASED

(dead) (The *c* has the "S" sound. Say "de-seest.") deceased _____

(sick) (The two *ss* have the "Z" sound. Say "di-zeezd.") diseased _____

Here is a spelling trick. Fill in the missing letters and then copy the trick into your notebook.

The *deCEASED* have *CEASED* to live.   The de_____ have _____ to live.

And remember that *diseased* can be broken down like this: *dis + ease + ed*

a. The doctor operated on the man's _____ heart.

b. She was alone in the world. All her relatives were _____.

c. The letter is not deliverable. The addressee is _____. (He's no longer living.)

11. DECENT—DESCENT

(proper; modest; kind) (The stress is on the first syllable. Say "DE-cent.")

decent _____

(a going down; decline) (The stress is on the second syllable. Say "deSCENT.")

descent _____

a. They are very _____ people.

b. The _____ of the plane was bumpy, but the landing was smooth.

c. He doesn't even have a _____ shirt to wear.

12. DESSERT—DESERT

Watch out! This pair is especially tricky. While there is one pronunciation and meaning for *dessert*, there are two different pronunciations and meanings for *desert*.

(after-dinner treat such as cake) (The stress is on the second syllable. Say "des-SERT.")

dessert _____

(to abandon) (The stress again is on the second syllable. Say "de-SERT.")

desert _____

(a sandy place with no trees or water) (The stress is on the first syllable. Say "DES-ert.")

desert _____

Here are some spelling tricks. Fill in the missing letters and copy the tricks into your notebook.

Please don't *DESERt* me in the *DESERt*. I don't *DESERve* it!

Please don't _____t me in the _____t. I don't _____ve it!

A *Sinfully Sweet deSSert*. A __infully __weet de__ert.

a. That was a great dinner. What's for _____?

b. The campers got lost in the _____.

c. Did he really _____ his wife and children?

d. I'm on a diet, so I have to skip _____.

13. ENVELOPE—ENVELOP

(a *noun* meaning a letter container) (The stress is on the first syllable. Say "EN-velope.")

envel**ope** _____

(a *verb* meaning to surround) (The stress is on the middle syllable. Say "en-VEL-op.")

envel**op** _____

a. Put the letter in the _____.

b. There was a manila _____ lying on the desk.

c. The fog seemed to _____ the city.

14. FOR—FOUR—FOURTEEN—FORTY

(a preposition) (Say "for" or "fer.") **for** _____

(4) **four** _____

(14) **four**teen _____

(40) **forty** _____

a. This is _____ you.

b. They have _____ children—two boys and two girls.

c. When my father turns _____, we'll throw a surprise party.

d. Thirteen, _____, fifteen.

15. MARITAL—MARTIAL

(related to marriage) (Say "mar-i-tal.") mar**ital** _____

(related to the military) (Say "mar-tial." (It sounds like "marshal.")

mar**tial** _____

a. They went to a marriage counselor because they were having _____ problems.

b. Are you interested in _____ arts like karate and kung fu?

c. The military took over the government and declared _____ law.

16. MORAL—MORALE

(*adjective:* right; *noun:* lesson, value, or principle) (Stress the first syllable. Say "MORal")

moral _____

(feeling of confidence and discipline) (Stress the second syllable. Say "morALE.")

mor**ale** _____

a. The _____ of the story is "Look before you leap."

b. Low employee _____ resulted in a low production rate.

c. Is it _____ to help someone commit suicide?

17. PERSONAL—PERSONNEL

(individual; private) (The stress is on the first syllable. Say "PERsonal.")

personal _____

(employees or staff) (The stress is on the last syllable. Say "personNEL.")

personnel _____

a. That's a very _____ question!

b. The _____ office is on the third floor.

c. She has her own _____ bodyguard.

18. QUIET—QUITE—QUIT

(not noisy) (This word has two syllables. Say "qui-et.") quiet _____

(very) (This word has one syllable and the "long I" sound. It rhymes with *bite*.)

quite _____

(stop or give up) (This word has the "short I" sound. It rhymes with *hit*.)

quit _____

a. You can save your own life if you _____ smoking.

b. Shhh! Please be _____ .

c. She's _____ nice, actually.

19. THOROUGH—THROUGH—THROUGHOUT—THOUGH—THOUGHT

Here are five words that are often confused. Let's work through each carefully. Read the definition and say the word out loud using the pronunciation hints in parentheses. Do the Say-Copy-Check exercise and then fill in the word in the sentence.

THOROUGH (complete) (Say "thor-o.") thorough _____

She did a _____ cleaning job.

THROUGH (in one side and out the other; done or finished.) (Say "throo.")

through _____

Let's walk _____ the park.

We're finally _____ with this project.

THROUGHOUT (all over; during the whole time) (Say "throo-out.")

throughout _____

NOTE: This word is simply *through* + *out*. She felt pain _____ her body.

_____ the lecture, he kept sneezing and blowing his nose.

THOUGH (however) (Say "tho.") though _____

He's handsome and well dressed. Watch out, _____ . He's dangerous.

THOUGHT (an idea; past tense of the verb *think*) (Say "thott.") thought _____

What are you doing here? I _____ you were in Las Vegas.

Here's a new _____ : let's sell the house and move to the country.

Now write the correct word: *thorough, through, throughout, though,* or *thought.*

a. Oh, it's only you! I _____ it was a burglar!

b. _____ his life, he suffered from alcoholism.

c. The children were dirty and disheveled. They were well behaved, _____.

d. They drove straight _____ the state without stopping.

e. You should have a _____ checkup.

PROOFREAD

Keep in mind everything you've learned about words that look almost alike. Find and correct the twenty errors below.

I learned a lot about my grandmother by reading her old dairy, which she kept throught her life. Let me tell you how I found it. While going thorough the attic one day, I came upon the little notebook stuck in a trunk alone with a lot of books and all her wedding cloths. I sat down and read all afternoon. It started out: "I am all along in the world. My grandparents and parents are all diseased. My only living relative is my aunt, but she desserted me. Now I live in an orphanage." Thirty pages later, the journal read: "I am so happy. I have been staying with Mr. and Mrs. Larson. Mr. Larson believes we must get up at 5:00 every morning, and Mrs. Larson believes we should eat spinach at every meal. But aside from these strange costumes, the Larsons are a kind, descent couple, and now they are going to adapt me."

Fourty pages later, the diary read: "I am now forteen years old. I have been quit ill lately. I fell down the stairs and hit my head. I was in a comma for a week. Now I am better, but the doctor says I need a through rest and must stay quite for several weeks." Thirty pages later, the book read: "I have met a wonderful young man—a perfect angle! His name is Rudolph." Not long after, the diary continued: "Rudolph and I have been married for five months now. Martial life has been good to me. Finally, I have a home of my own."

My grandmother grew up in that house and raised for children— three boys and a girl. She died before I was born, but after reading her diary, I felt as if I knew her.

Answers start on page 128.

Finding Confusing Words

The newspaper called me a thief, and I intend to sue for liable (?) libel (?)

Which word is correct? You know that both *liable* and *libel* are words, but how do you know the right one for the sentence? If you can't remember which word is which, turn to your dictionary and look each up. Read each definition carefully. Here is what you would find:

> **li·a·ble** (lī´ ə bəl) *adj.* 1. Legally obligated.
> 2. Subject to 3. Likely
> **li·bel** (lī´ bəl) *n.* 1. A written or printed statement
> that unjustly injures someone's reputation. 2. The
> act of publishing such a thing

After reading these definitions, choose the correct word for the sentence. _____

If you wrote *libel,* you were right. You wish to sue the newspaper for printing something that has injured you unjustly.

In the case of *liable* and *libel,* the definition is not the only difference. The pronunciation of the words is also different. (Compare the number of syllables in each.)

If the pronunciation symbols look funny to you, don't be concerned. Each dictionary uses a slightly different set of pronunciation symbols. These symbols are clearly explained at the beginning of the dictionary in a section marked "Pronunciation" or "Pronunciation Key." In addition, most dictionaries show examples of each symbol at the bottom of each page.

Once you have learned the symbols used by your dictionary, it's easy to see if you have the word you want by checking the pronunciation.

REMEMBER: If two words look or sound similar and you don't know when to use which, use your dictionary to check the *definition* and the *pronunciation.*

PRACTICE

Using your dictionary when you aren't sure, circle the correct word for each sentence.

a. The priest walked up to the _____.   altar   alter

b. They put a new dome on the _____.   capital   capitol

c. The restaurant served a _____ glass of wine with dinner.
   (It was free.)   complementary   complimentary

d. The advisory _____ met to draw up a list of
   guidelines.   council   counsel

e. The serpent _____ Eve astray.   lead   led

f. The coal _____ suffered from black lung disease.
   miner   minor

Answers start on page 128.

Words with *ALL* and *AL*

We've already (?) all ready (?) finished it.

Words with *al* and *all* can be tough. Do you know the correct spelling for the sentence above? If not, you'll find out soon if you work through the following exercises.

Two Words—Two Ls

ALL RIGHT

Although some dictionaries list *alright* as a nonstandard or disputed spelling, it's best to use the standard, accepted spelling, *all right*. These are two separate words. Do the Say-Copy-Check exercise:

*all right _____

Fill in the words: Are you _____ _____?

One Word—One L

ALMOST

This is one word with one *l*. Do the Say-Copy-Check exercise:

*almost _____

Fill in the word: I am _____ ready.

ALWAYS

This is one word with one *l*. Do the Say-Copy-Check exercise.

*always _____

Fill in the word: You are _____ late.

ALTHOUGH

This is one word with one *l*. Do the Say-Copy-Check exercise.

*although _____

Fill in the word: _____ he was rich, he was not happy.

ALREADY

This is one word with one *l*. Do the Say-Copy-Check exercise.

*already _____

Fill in the word: They have _____ washed the dishes.

Be careful. The single word *already* means "by this time." The words *all* and *ready* can be used separately as in this dialogue:

—We were *ready*.

—*All* of you?

—Yes. We were *all ready*.

Note that the two separate words *all* and *ready* have an entirely different meaning than *already* does. The final sentence means "*All* of us were *ready*."

A SPECIAL EXPRESSION: *A LOT*

Watch out. The expression *a lot*, meaning "very much," consists of two separate words. Do the Say-Copy-Check exercise.

*a lot _____

Fill in the words: I miss you ___ _____.

Write a sentence with *a lot*:

_____

PROOFREAD ———

Find and correct the seven errors below.

Although
~~All though~~ Ms. Johnson all most allways started class on time, three students—George, James and JoAnn—were late alot. On Monday, there was a test. By 8:30, most of the students were all ready done. At 8:35, George, James, and JoAnn walked in. "We're already for the test," they said. "Well, that's alright for you," said Ms. Johnson, "but we're all done!"

Answers start on page 129.

Dealing with Hard-to-Spell Names

Have you ever received a letter on which your name was misspelled? How did you feel about that? Imagine how a potential employer would feel if you spelled his or her name incorrectly in a letter of application. On the other hand, if you spell someone's name correctly, you'll make a good impression.

Here in the United States, there are all kinds of difficult names. That's because Americans have roots in languages all over the world. The spelling rules you study do not always apply to names from other languages. It would be impossible to learn the many thousands of different names. What can you do?

The only solution is to observe names carefully when you first see them. If possible, make up spelling tricks to help you remember.

Let's say you need to send your résumé and letter to someone named *Deborah Kaplansky*. Say the first and last names out loud as you study the spelling. You might mispronounce the name *Deborah* as "deBORah" to help you remember not to write the alternate spelling, *Debra*. (Of course, you should mispronounce the name only in order to learn it. Use the correct pronunciation when you address someone!)

Now for the last name. First divide it into syllables: *Ka-plan-sky*. To remember that the word starts with *k* (and not *c*), think of *OK:* "She's OK!" The second syllable is the word *plan,* and the third syllable looks like the word *sky* (even though it is pronounced "skee"). Can you remember the name now?

Write it here: _____

Try a harder name: *Ferdinand Ayckroyd* (pronounced "ak-roid"). Try the first name. Divide it into syllables: *Fer-din-and*. Say and study each syllable. It's not hard to learn this name since it is spelled as it sounds. The last name is harder. Divide it: *Ayck-royd*. The *a* is easy to remember because you can hear it pronounced clearly. To learn the rest of the first syllable, you could think of it as part of the call letters of a radio station: W*YCK* (if you live in the East) or K*YCK* (if you live in the West). Now you've got the *Ayck* of the name. For the second syllable, *royd,* you could think of Rolls *Roy*ce. Then all you have to do is remember the *d* to get *royd*.

Do you remember the name now?

Write it here: _____

Try your hand at these names. Divide them into syllables and think of spelling tricks for them, if possible. Then ask your instructor or someone else to dictate them to you, and see if you can spell them correctly.

a. Hilary Taylor

b. Roberto Esposito

c. Tamara Gaines

d. Sumiko Endo

e. Stanley Nowotarski

f. Anthea Tsoulos

g. Caryn Isenstein

h. Thanh Nguyen

i. Frederick Schmidt

j. Gina DiBrito

Review Test

Now test your knowledge of the confusing words that you have studied. Look at the clues in parentheses and write the correct complete word or words in the sentence. You will need to add one or more letters to the clues. The first one has been done for you.

a. Let's study the _____ on the Civil War.   (les—n)

b. He walked back and _____.   (f—th)

c. He paid her a _____ on her dramatic weight loss.   (compl—ent)

d. Don't _____ the chain.   (br—k)

e. She wrote a letter on company _____.   (station—ry)

f. She was thrilled when she _____ the test.   (pas—)

g. _____ gloves are these?   (Who—)

h. The bird flew back to _____ cage.   (it—)

i. —I come from Springfield.

    —Oh really? I do, _____!   (t—)

j. I can't _____ his apology.   (—cept)

k. Your whining won't _____ him in the least.   (—fect)

l. Did the post office ever _____ one of your letters?   (l—se)

m. Please _____ me on this matter.   (adv—e)

n. Whew! This bicycle is hard to _____.   (pe—l)

o. What is the function of this _____?   (dev—e)

p. We have a _____ staying at our house.   (gues—)

q. He is a good, _____ man.   (mor—)

r. Will they be able to _____ an infant?   (ad—pt)

s. I need some peace and _____.   (qu—t)

t. She prepared a chocolate cake for _____.   (des—t)

u. Dress up in your finest _____.   (clo—)

v. He left his job for _____ reasons.   (pers—l)

w. Look _____ the window.   (th—gh)

x. They've _____ been up for two hours.   (a—ready)

y. Keep going! You're _____ there!   (a—most)

Answers start on page 129.

You've finally finished the entire book! Now test your spelling knowledge.

Final Test

In each sentence, there may be a misspelled word. Circle the letter beneath the misspelled word. If all of the words are spelled correctly, circle (d) No misspelling.

Example:

The boss was <u>uncommonly</u> <u>dissatisfied</u> with the <u>counsselor's</u> work. <u>No misspelling</u>.
  a   b   ⓒ   d

1. She didn't want to <u>aknowledge</u> that in the <u>absence</u> of studying, her <u>academic</u> grades had fallen.
                       a   b   c
   <u>No misspelling</u>.
   d

2. She was <u>embarrased</u> that she had discontinued her <u>education</u> in the <u>eighth</u> grade. <u>No misspelling</u>.
            a   b   c   d

3. The American Medical Association is <u>advertizing</u> <u>against</u> <u>cigarettes</u>. <u>No misspelling</u>.
                                       a   b   c   d

4. It is <u>definite</u> that the <u>engineer</u> will be <u>availible</u> for the job. <u>No misspelling</u>.
         a   b   c   d

5. The convict is an <u>eligible</u> <u>candidate</u> for <u>capitol</u> punishment. <u>No misspelling</u>.
                     a   b   c   d

6. My <u>nephew</u> has a good <u>memory</u>, so he is studying <u>medecine</u>. <u>No misspelling</u>.
      a   b   c   d

7. The <u>author</u> has a book on <u>choclate</u> being published in the <u>autumn</u>. <u>No misspelling</u>.
       a   b   c   d

8. The Deere <u>Corporation</u> <u>manufachures</u> <u>machinery</u>. <u>No misspelling</u>.
             a   b   c   d

9. They took great <u>delite</u> in riding in a <u>private</u> <u>carriage</u>. <u>No misspelling</u>.
                   a   b   c   d

10. Her dad is going to <u>purchase</u> a new <u>bicycle</u> for her because a <u>burgler</u> stole her last one. <u>No</u>
                        a   b   c
    <u>misspelling</u>.
    d

11. <u>Allthough</u> she was an <u>excellent</u> <u>professor</u>, her salary was low. <u>No misspelling</u>.
    a   b   c   d

12. The <u>sargeant's</u> mind hung in the <u>balance</u> before his last major <u>campaign</u>. <u>No misspelling</u>.
        a   b   c   d

13. The <u>famous</u> bar had its <u>liqour</u> <u>license</u> revoked. <u>No misspelling</u>.
        a   b   c   d

14. <u>Attendance</u> was <u>average</u> but the <u>audiance</u> was awful. <u>No misspelling</u>.
    a   b   c   d

15. The <u>psycholigist</u> had a good <u>reference</u> and was <u>reliable</u>. <u>No misspelling</u>.
        a   b   c   d

16. My brother's <u>supervisor</u> is an <u>ignorent</u> <u>hypocrite</u>. <u>No misspelling</u>.
                 a   b   c   d

17. We bought a <u>beutiful</u> <u>bouquet</u> to brighten the house for the <u>holiday</u>. <u>No misspelling</u>.
                a   b   c   d

18. She sent for a <u>goverment</u> <u>pamphlet</u> on <u>tenant</u> rights. <u>No misspelling</u>.
                   a   b   c   d

19. Both <u>science</u> and <u>literature</u> should be studied in <u>school</u>. <u>No misspelling</u>.
         a   b   c   d

20. Marco isn't <u>unnatural</u> or <u>peculiar</u>, he's just <u>original</u>. <u>No misspelling</u>.
                a   b   c   d

21. He kept the <u>guitar</u> as a <u>souvenier</u> of his <u>travels</u>. <u>No misspelling</u>.
                a   b   c   d

22. Jay's is a great <u>restaurant</u>—you can get a <u>salad</u> and a <u>sanwich</u> for $2. <u>No misspelling</u>.
                     a   b   c   d

23. With your talent, you should <u>pursue</u> a <u>career</u> in <u>buisness</u>. <u>No misspelling</u>.
                                 a   b   c   d

24. I have a <u>busy</u> <u>schedule</u>, so I'll call you back <u>tommorow</u>. <u>No misspelling</u>.
             a   b   c   d

25. <u>Pronunciation</u> <u>exercises</u> <u>develope</u> your speaking ability. <u>No misspelling</u>.
    a   b   c   d

26. What an <u>extraordinary</u> <u>individual</u> our <u>governer</u> is! <u>No misspelling</u>.
           a   b   c   d

27. Some writers use <u>humor</u> or <u>gimmicks</u> to keep the reader's <u>intrest</u>. <u>No misspelling</u>.
               a   b   c   d

28. The train <u>conductor</u> was <u>pleasant</u> and <u>curteous</u> even though we didn't have tickets. <u>No misspelling</u>.
           a   b   c   d

29. The <u>plumber</u> and the <u>mechanic</u> came to look at the <u>damage</u>. <u>No misspelling</u>.
        a   b   c   d

30. His <u>philosophy</u> about <u>marrage</u> is, be <u>optimistic</u>. <u>No misspelling</u>.
        a   b   c   d

31. Just <u>between</u> you and me, that <u>amateur</u> <u>athelete</u> has two left feet. <u>No misspelling</u>.
        a   b   c   d

32. The <u>library</u> is across from the <u>grocery</u> store and the <u>laundramat</u>. No misspelling.
        a   b   c   d

33. The <u>villian</u> stole the queen's <u>diamond</u> <u>jewelry</u>. No <u>misspelling</u>.
        a   b   c   d

34. Don't be <u>ankshus</u>! Stay <u>calm</u>, and we'll get to the <u>bottom</u> of this. No <u>misspelling</u>.
        a   b   c   d

35. Take the baby to the <u>hospital</u> if his <u>cogh</u> worsens or his <u>temperature</u> goes up. No <u>misspelling</u>.
               a   b   c   d

36. The <u>president</u> declared the situation an <u>official</u> <u>crisis</u>. No misspelling.
        a   b   c

37. The judge's <u>decision</u> gave the mother <u>custady</u> of the <u>eight-year-old</u> boy. No misspelling.
           a   b   c   d

38. I <u>suggest</u> that you <u>vaccum</u> before the <u>visitor</u> arrives. No <u>misspelling</u>.
      a   b   c   d

39. We have <u>enough</u> <u>fashon</u> <u>magazines</u> to wallpaper this apartment. No <u>misspelling</u>.
           a   b   c   d

40. This <u>conveniant</u> <u>knife</u> was a <u>bargain</u>. No misspelling.
        a   b   c   d

41. You're in <u>trouble</u> <u>again</u>, <u>yung</u> man! <u>No misspelling</u>.
           a   b   c   d

42. This <u>country's</u> economy will collapse <u>because</u> of our national debt. No misspelling.
        a   b   c   d

43. I <u>use to</u> <u>quarrel</u> with my <u>rival</u> all the time. No misspelling.
      a   b   c   d

44. Our <u>labratory</u> <u>equipment</u> isn't <u>sufficient</u>. No misspelling.
        a   b   c   d

45. He may be <u>intellegent</u>, but he's too <u>stubborn</u> to accept a new <u>theory</u>. No misspelling.
          a   b   c   d

46. Our <u>ancesters</u> lived in these <u>mountains</u> and <u>valleys</u>. No misspelling.
        a   b   c   d

47. It's <u>horrible</u>, but <u>acidents</u> do happen. No <u>misspelling</u>.
        a   b   c   d

48. Are you <u>certain</u> that this buffalo nickel is the <u>genuine</u> <u>artical</u>? No misspelling.
          a   b   c   d

49. The <u>bulletin</u> from the <u>Citezin's</u> <u>Bureau</u> came today. No <u>misspelling</u>.
        a   b   c   d

50. She has the <u>necesary</u> <u>confidence</u> and <u>courage</u> to be a firefighter. <u>No misspelling</u>.
          a   b   c   d

Answers start on page 129.

Answer Key

Diagnostic Test

1. susceptible
2. advertise
3. technique
4. dilemma
5. embarrass
6. exhibit
7. subtle
8. mortgage
9. fatigue
10. nuisance
11. marriage
12. sergeant
13. neutral
14. gasoline
15. Environment
16. twelfth
17. miniature
18. magazine
19. temperature
20. accident
21. Saturday
22. ignorant
23. responsible
24. capital
25. prejudice
26. wrote
27. said
28. told
29. bought
30. caught
31. were
32. shook
33. fought
34. thought
35. swept
36. done
37. taken
38. written
39. been
40. known
41. altar
42. compliment
43. aisle
44. accept
45. picture
46. effect
47. clothes
48. dessert
49. through
50. comma

Introduction to Spelling Skills

page 3   Practice 1
a. against
b. tenant
c. acknowledge
d. standard

Proofread

page 4   Practice 2

My brother is a **tenant** in a lovely North Shore apartment building. His **annual** lease will expire in February. He signed a **standard** lease that **acknowledges** no increase in the rate of his rent. He will probably renew his lease since he **prefers** to maintain a reasonable rent rate.

SECTION 1

Special Consonant Sounds 1: "S" Sound

page 6   Practice 1
a. citizen
b. license
c. medicine
d. city
e. ancestor
f. absence
g. necessary
h. source
i. grocery
j. society
k. circle

page 7   Practice 2
a. susceptible
b. scissors
c. scene
d. fascinate
e. muscle
f. discipline

Special Consonant Sounds 2: "Z" Sound

page 9   Practice 1
a. presence
b. pleasant
c. wisdom
d. criticism
e. visible
f. scissors
g. possession

page 9   Practice 2
a. exercise
b. recognize
c. criticize
d. apologize
e. surprise
f. advertise
g. analyze

page 10   Proofread
a. wisdom
b. OK
c. surprise
d. OK
e. exercise
f. visible
g. apologize
h. OK
i. criticism
j. analyze
k. advertise
l. OK

Special Consonant Sounds 3: "SH" Sound

page 12   Practice 1
a. prediction
b. education
c. permission
d. corporation
e. admission
f. partial

page 12   Practice 2
a. musician
b. financial
c. sufficient
d. precious
e. physician
f. official
g. special

page 13   Practice 3
a. sure
b. insurance
c. ocean
d. machine

page 13   Proofread
a. precious
b. OK
c. insurance
d. OK
e. financial
f. corporation
g. delicious
h. machine
i. OK
j. physician

Special Consonant Sounds 4: "CH" Sound

page 14   Practice
a. actually
b. future
c. signature
d. temperature
e. unnatural
f. manufacture
g. amateur

Special Consonant Sounds 5: "ZH" Sound

page 16   Practice
a. usually
b. decision
c. seizure
d. leisure
e. measure
f. confusion
g. occasional

Special Consonant Sounds 6: "J" Sound

page 17   Practice 1
a. general
b. generous
c. vegetable
d. apologize
e. genuine
f. tragedy

page 18   Practice 2
a. soldier
b. education
c. schedule
d. procedure
e. gradually
f. individual

page 18   Proofread
a. generous
b. OK
c. soldier
d. schedule
e. OK
f. vegetable
g. procedure
h. OK
i. individual

Special Consonant Sounds 7: "F" Sound

page 19   Practice 1
a. physician
b. physical
c. nephew
d. pamphlet
e. telephone
f. phobia
g. philosophy

page 20   Practice 2
a. tough
b. rough
c. laugh
d. enough
e. cough

page 20   Proofread
a. phobia
b. enough
c. nephew
d. philosophy
e. physician
f. fly

Special Consonant Sounds 8: "K" Sound

page 22   Proofread

Dr. Sonya Biggs is a **psychologist** at Denter High **School,** where she has a very busy **schedule.** Although few students have real **character** disorders, there are many students who have less serious **psychological** problems. Some students abuse drugs or **liquor,** and Dr. Biggs uses a variety of **techniques** to treat them. Other students have problems at home. Even though Dr. Biggs often goes home with a **headache,** she wouldn't give up her work for the world.

Looking Up Spellings

page 24   Practice
a. major
b. trough
c. arise
d. ceiling
e. pleasure
f. gentle
g. chronic
h. mystique
i. plaque
j. toxin
k. alley
l. hallucinate

Double Consonants: FF

page 25   Practice
a. different
b. sufficient
c. official
d. efficient

Double Consonants: LL

page 27   Practice
a. valley
b. dollar
c. allow
d. intelligent
e. fulfillment
f. balloons

Double Consonants: MM

page 27 Practice

a. summary
b. grammar
c. dilemma
d. gimmick

Double Consonants: RR

page 28 Practice

a. horrible
b. terrible
c. tomorrow
d. interrupt
e. quarrel
f. embarrass

Double Consonants: SS

page 29 Practice

a. possible
b. professor
c. message
d. possession

page 30 Crossword Puzzle

page 30 Proofread

a. aggressive
b. embarrass
c. cigarette
d. tomorrow
e. bulletin
f. fulfillment
g. professor
h. necessary

Silent Consonants: B

page 32 Practice

a. debt
b. plumber
c. subtle
d. doubt
e. undoubtedly

Silent Consonants: GH

page 33 Practice

a. delight
b. height
c. tonight
d. straight
e. eight
f. eighth

Silent Consonants: H

page 33 Practice

a. honor
b. exhibit
c. rhyme
d. heir
e. rhythm
f. exhausted

Silent Consonants: K

page 34 Practice

a. knowledge
b. knot
c. knob
d. knee
e. knife

Silent Consonants: P

page 34 Practice

a. psalm
b. psychologist
c. psychological
d. psychiatrist
e. receipt

Silent Consonants: W

page 35 Practice

a. Wrap
b. Answer
c. Wring
d. acknowledge

Silent Consonants: Mixed

page 35 Practice

a. autumn
b. February
c. Fasten
d. solemn
e. calm
f. campaign
g. Wednesday

Review of Consonants

page 36

a. tomorrow
b. OK
c. enough
d. answer
e. OK
f. mortgage
g. Wednesday
h. necessary
i. OK
j. analyze
k. OK
l. signature
m. seizure
n. procedure
o. physical
p. mechanic
q. liquor
r. OK
s. acknowledge
t. psychological
u. OK
v. receipt
w. straight

A Letter of Thanks

page 37 Proofread

161 Esperanza Dr.
San Diego, CA 92120

Mrs. Estela Herrera
Personnel Director
Seaview Bank
1400 Ridgeway Rd.
San Diego, CA 92136

Dear Mrs. Herrera:

I would like to express my **appreciation** for the **opportunity** you gave me to learn more about the teller position at Seaview Bank and to tell you about my own background. After the **interview,** my **interest** in working at your bank is even stronger than before.

If I can **provide** any **further information** about my qualifications, please do not **hesitate** to **contact** me.

Again, thank you for your time and **attention.**

Sincerely,
Lisa Wolek

SECTION 2

Silent Vowels: A

page 39 Practice

a. pleasant
b. measure
c. diamond
d. jealous
e. dial

Silent Vowels: I

page 39 Practice

a. marriage
b. fashion
c. nuisance
d. carriage

Silent Vowels: U

page 39 Practice

a. guitar
b. build
c. guidance
d. fatigue
e. guarantee

page 40 Proofread

a. straight
b. OK
c. Wednesday
d. plumber
e. OK
f. solemn
g. psychological
h. OK
i. undoubtedly
j. February
k. knot
l. OK
m. fasten
n. campaign
o. guitar
p. OK
q. rhythm
r. subtle
s. OK

Letter to a School

page 41 Proofread

1212 Rainbow Dr.
Colonia, NJ 07067
July 22, 1986

Ms. Alma L. Robinson
Director of **Admissions**
Fordham **Community College**
8300 Lynn Pl.
Colonia, NJ 07067

Dear Ms. Robinson:

I am a recent GED **graduate** seeking information regarding admission to your air conditioning and refrigeration **program.** I also have an **interest** in the electronics and **computer certificates** offered through your **college** and am anxious to know more about your **curriculum.** Would it be possible to have a **schedule** of fall **courses,** a **catalogue,** and an **application** form sent to me?

I spoke with the **dean** last week, and he indicated that since I am a veteran and will be a **degree**-seeking student I would be **eligible** for **financial assistance.** Please send me the **appropriate** form to apply for this aid.

Thank you for your attention.

Sincerely,
Carrie Lovett

SPELLING DOESN'T MATCH PRONUNCIATION

Unusual Vowel Spellings

page 42   Practice 1
a. against
b. again
c. again
d. against

page 43   Practice 2
a. young
b. country
c. tongue
d. trouble

page 43   Practice 3
a. maneuver
b. neutral

Words from French

page 44   Practice 1
a. bureau
b. beauty
c. beautiful
d. bureaucracy

page 44   Practice 2
a. souvenir
b. technique
c. gasoline
d. machine
e. fatigue

page 45   Practice 3
a. gauge
b. bouquet

Other Difficult Spellings

page 45   Practice
a. foreign
b. vacuum
c. anxious
d. recipe

page 45   Scrambled Words
a. AGAIN
b. RECIPE
c. VACUUM
d. BUSY
e. FOREIGN
f. GAUGE
g. TONGUE
h. BUREAU
i. YOUNG
j. NEUTRAL
k. SERGEANT

page 46   Proofread
a. anxious
b. business
c. bouquet
d. OK
e. foreign
f. courteous
g. Bureau
h. gasoline
i. OK
j. beautiful
k. sergeant
l. souvenir

SPELLING AND PRONUNCIATION

ING Ending

page 48   Proofread
As I was **walking** out of my house this **morning,** I saw the mail carrier **coming** up the street **pushing** her cart. As she passed my neighbors' house, their dog came **running** out, **barking** his head off. He jumped over the fence, ran up to the mail carrier, and began **growling** and **snapping** at her. The mail carrier kept **going** down the street, but I could see she was **pulling** a can of Mace out of her pocket. She didn't have to use it, though, because the dog stopped **chasing** her as soon as he saw she wasn't scared. The mail carrier said to me, "That's been **happening** too much lately." I said, "Don't worry—all I've got is a canary, and it doesn't bite!"

ED Adjectives

page 49   Practice
a. supposed
b. tired
c. used
d. prejudiced
e. closed
f. shocked
g. messed
h. surprised

Final Consonant Sounds

page 50   Proofread
I have a lot of **respect** for my neighbor, Kiet, from Viet Nam. He has just opened a **restaurant** that serves food from his country. This is his **first attempt** at a business, and I hope it's not too big a **risk.** He works very hard, though, and the food is delicious. Also, Kiet **strictly** follows health regulations in food preparation.

Kiet and his wife work twelve hours a day at the **restaurant.** Their children give them a **hand** on the weekends, but Kiet hasn't **asked** them to give up their studies—he thinks education is too important. I wish Kiet the **best** of luck, and I **suggest** that you try the food at his place soon.

Letter Reversal

page 51   Practice
a. perspire
b. jewelry
c. secretary
d. hundred
e. prescription
f. nuclear
g. environment
h. pursue

Letter Omission

page 53   Proofread
a. OK
b. OK
c. government
d. recognize
e. library
f. length
g. representative
h. OK
i. quantity
j. sandwich
k. OK
l. peculiar
m. vehicle

Extra Letters and Syllables

page 54   Proofread
Harry committed a **grievous** crime: he stole the team mascot. Now, Harry was a **mischievous** young man who loved to play practical jokes. One day, while all the other **athletes** were on the field, Harry snuck into the locker room. He searched through all the **equipment** until he found Gladys the goose—a toy that was the mascot of the Flapping Geese football team. With Gladys in a sack slung across his shoulder, Harry made his **escape.** No one noticed Gladys's absence until Harry innocently announced that he had received a ransom note, which he read aloud with exaggerated **pronunciation:** "Give me the goods, or Gladys gets it!" The team was on to Harry and didn't buy the kidnapping story. They stormed Harry's locker and found Gladys under a pile of dirty sweatshirts.

Review of Silent Vowels & Pronunciation Errors

page 55
a. athlete
b. OK
c. OK
d. because
e. environment
f. OK
g. sergeant
h. government
i. jewelry
j. OK
k. courage
l. probably
m. OK
n. OK
o. recognize
p. OK
q. sandwich
r. OK
s. strength
t. strictly
u. supposed
v. anxious
w. OK

Reduced Vowel Roots 1: A

page 57   Proofread
a. academic
b. OK
c. extraordinary
d. explanation
e. magazine
f. OK
g. representative
h. senator
i. separate
j. OK

Reduced Vowel Roots 2: E

page 59 Proofread

a. bulletin
b. maintenance
c. OK
d. tragedy
e. vegetable
f. cemetery
g. OK
h. benefits
i. elevator
j. OK
k. enemy
l. repetition
m. specific

Reduced Vowel Roots 3: ER

page 60 Practice

a. preference
b. interest
c. conference
d. temperature
e. governor
f. average
g. literature
h. general
i. desperate

Reduced Vowel Roots 4: I

page 61 Practice

a. fascinate
b. accident
c. coincidence
d. cigar
e. candidate
f. alibi
g. definite
h. engineer
i. eligible
j. evident

page 62 Proofread

a. repetitive
b. optimistic
c. OK
d. privilege
e. responsibility
f. OK
g. medicine
h. holiday
i. OK
j. original

Reduced Vowel Roots 5: O

page 63 Practice

a. innocent
b. laundromat
c. opinion
d. custody
e. apologize
f. gasoline
g. customer
h. opposite
i. hypocrite
j. chocolate

Reduced Vowel Roots 6: OR

page 64 Proofread

a. favorite
b. OK
c. laboratory
d. opportunity

Reduced Vowel Roots 7: U

page 65 Practice

a. prejudice
b. Saturday
c. volunteer
d. luxury

page 66 Proofread

In **general,** when it comes to ideal living quarters, most people have a **definite preference.** Some people would like to live in a **luxury** high-rise. In a high-rise, you never have to climb stairs because there is an **elevator.** You never have to haul your clothes to the **laundromat** because there's a laundry room in the building. Many buildings also have **separate** storage rooms, **bicycle** rooms, and party rooms. Some even have their own **restaurants.** And since the building has a full-time **maintenance** staff, you never have to worry about hiring a plumber, carpenter, or painter.

Other people would rather have their own home in the suburbs. Even though you must take full **responsibility** for the upkeep of the house, you have many **benefits.** You have more privacy, and you can play your **favorite** music as loud as you want without disturbing your neighbors. You have your own big yard to relax in—if you don't mind spending **Saturday** mowing the lawn! And you may feel that a real house seems more **permanent** than an apartment.

Of course, most of us don't have the **privilege** of choosing the ideal living situation, but we can always dream.

Reduced Vowel Suffixes 1: ENT/ENCE and ANT/ANCE

page 68 Proofread 1

a. audience
b. apparent
c. maintenance
d. tenant
e. preference
f. guidance

page 69 Proofread 2

a. significance
b. absent
c. evidence
d. instance
e. dependent
f. assistant
g. permanence
h. ignorance
i. presence
j. obedience

Reduced Vowel Suffixes 2: OR and AR

page 71 Practice 1

a. author
b. odor
c. conductor
d. elevator
e. governor
f. honor
g. counselor
h. ancestor
i. calculator
j. humor

page 71 Practice 2

a. professor
b. senator
c. survivor
d. visitor
e. radiator
f. sponsor
g. supervisor
h. spectator

page 72 Practice 3

a. popular
b. familiar
c. dollar
d. particular
e. calendar
f. peculiar
g. similar
h. burglar
i. grammar,

page 72 Proofread

a. author
b. burglar
c. visitor
d. dollar
e. calendar
f. spectator
g. odor

Reduced Vowel Suffixes 3: ABLE/IBLE

page 73 Practice

a. returnable
b. terrible
c. horrible
d. washable
e. acceptable
f. eligible
g. reliable
h. visible
i. adorable
j. desirable
k. possible
l. incredible
m. profitable
n. susceptible
o. suitable
p. available

page 74 Proofread

a. horrible
b. visible
c. desirable
d. OK
e. inevitable
f. responsible
g. OK
h. flexible
i. suitable
j. reversible
k. indispensable

Reduced Vowel Suffixes 4: LE/EL/AL

page 75 Practice 1

a. circle
b. bottle
c. article
d. trouble
e. muscle
f. vehicle

page 76 Practice 2

a. occasional
b. physical
c. neutral
d. hospital
e. rival
f. proposal
g. practical
h. official

page 77 Proofread

a. practical
b. general
c. OK
d. hospital
e. article
f. rival
g. OK
h. model
i. symbol

Reduced Vowel Suffixes 5: ARY/ERY/ORY

page 78 Practice 1

a. dictionary
b. necessary
c. boundary
d. ordinary
e. summary
f. secretary

page 79 Practice 2

a. grocery
b. machinery
c. Cemetery
d. stationery

page 79 Proofread

a. summary
b. history
c. OK
d. secretary
e. necessary
f. OK
g. machinery
h. stationery
i. OK
j. memory

Reduced Vowel Suffixes 6: AIN/ON/OM

page 80 Practice 1

a. mountain
b. bargain
c. villain
d. certain

page 80 Practice 2

a. common
b. Pardon
c. wagon
d. opinion
e. wisdom
f. poison

Reduced Vowel Suffixes 7: ACY/ASY

page 81 Proofread

a. fantasy b. OK c. Hypocrisy d. ecstasy e. privacy

Reduced Vowel Suffixes 8: Tricky Endings

page 83   Proofread 1

a. purchase
b. OK
c. salad
d. develop
e. OK
f. furnace
g. prejudice
h. OK
i. crisis
j. damage

page 83   Proofread 2

   The **tenant** upstairs is rather strange. Because he's always afraid a **burglar** will break into his house, he decided to **purchase** bars for his door. That in itself is not strange, but these bars are **permanent**—they don't open, so he has to climb through the window. Once inside, he puts rat **poison** on the window ledge, although I don't know why he thinks that will deter anyone from entering.

   I was shocked when he actually went away on a three-day vacation. During his **absence,** he left on a tape recording that continuously played the sound of a dog barking. He didn't ask me or my neighbors to look after his place. He is **certainly** not a friendly man. He has tacked up a marked **calendar** and a piece of personal **stationery** that says: "**Visitors:** Please sign up in advance. I'm only **available** on the indicated days. I value my **privacy.**" I'll bet you no one has ever signed up!

Getting Lost in Words

page 84   Practice

a. Declaration
b. familiar
c. definition
d. advantage
e. fascinating
f. specific
g. temperature
h. athlete
i. enemy

Past Tense and Past Participles

page 87   Practice 1

a. read
b. slept
c. felt
d. left
e. cost
f. spent
g. bought
h. saw
i. thought
j. told
k. wrote
l. spoke
m. took
n. drank
o. began
p. forgot
q. paid

page 88   Practice 2

a. said
b. led
c. felt
d. taught
e. fought
f. written
g. ridden
h. chosen
i. stolen
j. known
k. eaten
l. fallen
m. gotten
n. hidden
o. been

page 89   Practice 3

a. bent
b. sold
c. shot
d. lost
e. written
f. broken
g. frozen
h. stolen
i. worn
j. torn
k. sworn
l. shaken
m. drunk

Finding Difficult Past Forms and Past Participles

page 90   Practice

a. break–broke–broken
b. know–knew–known
c. lead–led–led
d. feel–felt–felt
e. drink–drank–drunk
f. tell–told–told

Review Test

page 91   Review

a. representative
b. bulletin
c. written
d. tragedy
e. temperature
f. custody
g. laundromat
h. laboratory
i. brought
j. volunteer
k. apparent
l. vengeance
m. superintendent
n. calendar
o. survivors
p. indispensable
g. vehicle
r. ordinary
s. said
t. poison
u. ecstasy
v. purchase

SECTION 3

Words that Sound Alike

page 92–99

1. a. aloud
    b. allowed
    c. allowed
2. a. alter
    b. altar
    c. alter
3. a. bass
    b. base
    c. base
4. a. birth
    b. berth
    c. birth
5. a. brake
    b. break
    c. break
6. a. capital
    b. capitol
    c. capital
    d. capital
    e. capital
7. a. serial
    b. cereal
    c. serial
8. a. kernel
    b. kernel
    c. colonel
9. a. complement
    b. compliment
    c. compliment
    d. complimentary
    e. complementary
    f. complimentary
10. a. cord
    b. chord
    c. cord
11. a. counsel
    b. council
    c. counsel
    d. counselor
12. a. fair
    b. fare
    c. fair
13. a. fourth
    b. fourth
    c. forth
14. a. heal
    b. heel
    c. heal
15. a. hear
    b. here
    c. hear
16. a. horse
    b. horse
    c. hoarse
17. a. hole
    b. whole
    c. whole
18. a. isle
    b. aisle
    c. aisle
19. a. led
    b. lead
    c. led
20. a. lessen
    b. lesson
    c. lesson
21. a. meet
    b. meet
    c. meat
22. a. miner
    b. minor
    c. minor
23. a. naval
    b. navel
    c. naval
24. a. past
    b. passed
    c. passed
25. a. pole
    b. poll
    c. pole
26. a. pore
    b. pour
    c. pore
27. a. principle
    b. principal
    c. principal
28. a. profit
    b. profit
    c. prophet
29. a. Roll
    b. roll
    c. role
    d. roll
30. a. steak
    b. stake
    c. stake
31. a. stationery
    b. stationary
    c. stationery
32. a. to
    b. two
    c. too
    d. too
    e. to
33. a. vain
    b. vein
    c. vain
34. a. waste
    b. waist
    c. waste

page 99   Proofread

a. alter
b. birth
c. break
d. OK
e. counseling
   OR counselling
f. fair
g. OK
h. whole
i. OK
j. minor
k. passed
l. OK
m. stationery
n. waste
o. fourth
p. allowed

Contractions and Possessives

page 100   Practice 1

a. Who is going to help me?
   Who's going to help me?
b. It is my favorite show.
   It's my favorite show.
c. I don't know what they are doing.
   I don't know what they're doing.
d. He says that you are a good cook.
   He says that you're a good cook.
e. I have a friend who is seven feet tall.
   I have a friend who's seven feet tall.

page 100   Practice 2

a. Whose
b. your
c. their
d. whose
e. its

page 101   Practice 3

a. Who's
b. Whose
c. who's
d. whose

page 101   Practice 4
a. It's   c. it's
b. its   d. its

page 101   Practice 5
a. your   c. you're
b. You're   d. your

page 101   Practice 6
a. they're   c. Their
b. They're   d. their

page 102   Practice 7
a. there   c. Their
b. They're   d. There

page 103   Proofread
a. OK   g. your
b. You're   h. OK
c. its   i. who's
d. OK   j. They're
e. whose   k. it's
f. their   l. There

Words that Sound Almost Alike
pages 104–108

1. a. accept
   b. except
   c. accept
2. a. addition
   b. edition
   c. Addition
3. a. advise
   b. advice
   c. advice
4. a. affect
   b. effect
   c. affect
   d. affect
   e. effect
5. a. bury
   b. berry
   c. bury
6. a. conscience
   b. conscious
   c. conscientious

7. a. device
   b. devise
   c. device
8. a. formally
   b. Formerly
   c. formally
9. a. Guess
   b. guest
   c. guess
10. a. allusion
    b. illusion
    c. illusion
11. a. liable
    b. liable
    c. libel
12. a. loose
    b. lose
    c. lose
13. a. metal
    b. medal

c. metal
d. meddle
14. a. pedal
    b. peddle
    c. petal
    d. pedal
15. a. picture
    b. pitcher
    c. pitcher
    d. picture
16. a. precede
    b. proceed
    c. proceed
17. a. weather
    b. whether
    c. whether

page 108   Proofread
a. addition   f. formerly
b. accept   g. guest
c. advice   h. lose
d. OK   i. metal
e. device   j. preceding

A Letter of Complaint
page 109   Proofread
Dear Sir or Madam:

Yesterday I **received** a bill from your company for $25.99. I **paid** this bill last month and am **enclosing** a copy of the **cancelled** (**OR canceled**) check to prove it. Please **credit** my account accordingly. Thank you for your **attention.**

Sincerely,
Louis Richardson

Dear Sir or Madam:

I ordered a set of cookware from you six months ago. It finally arrived yesterday, but it was **defective.** Two of the pots were **missing,** and the frying pan was **damaged.** I am returning the set to you and would **appreciate** a complete **refund** as soon as possible.

Yours truly,
Teresa Alvarez Ochoa

Words that Look Almost Alike
page 110–114

1. a. adapt
   b. adopt
   c. adopt
2. a. ally
   b. alley
   c. ally
3. a. along
   b. alone
   c. alone
4. a. angle
   b. angle
   c. angel
5. a. breathe
   b. breath
   c. breathe
6. a. close
   b. clothes
   c. cloth
7. a. coma
   b. comma

8. a. custom
   b. custom
   c. costume
9. a. diary
   b. dairy
   c. diary
10. a. diseased
    b. deceased
    c. deceased
11. a. decent
    b. descent
    c. decent
12. a. dessert
    b. desert
    c. desert
    d. dessert
13. a. envelope
    b. envelope
    c. envelop

14. a. for
    b. four
    c. forty
    d. fourteen
15. a. marital
    b. martial
    c. martial
16. a. moral
    b. morale
    c. moral
17. a. personal
    b. personnel
    c. personal
18. a. quit
    b. quiet
    c. quite
19. a. thought
    b. Throughout
    c. though
    d. through
    e. thorough

Page 115   Proofread

I learned a lot about my grandmother by reading her old **diary,** which she kept **throughout** her life. Let me tell you how I found it. While going **through** the attic one day, I came upon the little notebook stuck in a trunk **along** with a lot of books and all her wedding **clothes.** I sat down and read all afternoon. It started out: "I am all **alone** in the world. My grandparents and parents are all **deceased.** My only living relative is my aunt, but she **deserted** me. Now I live in an orphanage." Thirty pages later, the journal read: "I am so happy. I have been staying with Mr. and Mrs. Larson. Mr. Larson believes we must get up at 5:00 every morning, and Mrs. Larson believes we should eat spinach at every meal. But aside from these strange **customs,** the Larsons are a kind, **decent** couple, and now they are going to **adopt** me."

Forty pages later, the diary read: "I am now **fourteen** years old. I have been **quite** ill lately. I fell down the stairs and hit my head. I was in a **coma** for a week. Now I am better, but the doctor says I need a **thorough** rest and must stay **quiet** for several weeks." Thirty pages later, the book read: "I have met a wonderful young man—a perfect **angel!** His name is Rudolph." Not long after, the diary continued: "Rudolph and I have been married for five months now. **Marital** life has been good to me. Finally, I have a home of my own."

My grandmother grew up in that house and raised **four** children—three boys and a girl. She died before I was born, but after reading her diary, I felt as if I knew her.

Finding Confusing Words
page 116   Practice
a. altar   d. council
b. capitol   e. led
c. complimentary   f. miner

Words with *ALL* and *AL*

page 118 Proofread

Although Ms. Johnson **almost always** started class on time, three students—George, James, and JoAnn—were late **a lot.** On Monday, there was a test. By 8:30, most of the students were **already** done. At 8:35, George, James, and JoAnn walked in. "We're **all ready** for the test," they said. "Well, that's **all right** for you," said Ms. Johnson, "but we're **all done!**"

Review Test

page 120

a. lesson
b. forth
c. compliment
d. break
e. stationery
f. passed
g. whose
h. its
i. too
j. accept
k. affect
l. lose
m. advise
n. pedal
o. device
p. guest
q. moral
s. quiet
t. dessert
u. clothes
v. personal
w. through
x. already
y. almost

Final Test

pages 121–122

1. (a) acknowledge
2. (a) embarrassed
3. (a) advertising
4. (c) available
5. (c) capital
6. (c) medicine
7. (b) chocolate
8. (b) manufactures
9. (a) delight
10. (c) burglar
11. (a) Although
12. (a) sergeants
13. (b) liquor
14. (c) audience
15. (a) psychologist
16. (b) ignorant
17. (a) beautiful
18. (a) government
19. (d) No misspelling
20. (d) No misspelling
21. (b) souvenir
22. (c) sandwich
23. (c) business
24. (c) tomorrow
25. (c) develop
26. (c) governor
27. (c) interest
28. (c) courteous
29. (d) No misspelling
30. (b) marriage
31. (c) athlete
32. (c) laundromat
33. (a) villain
34. (a) anxious
35. (b) cough
36. (d) No misspelling
37. (b) custody
38. (b) vacuum
39. (b) fashion
40. (a) convenient
41. (c) young
42. (d) No misspelling
43. (a) used to
44. (a) laboratory
45. (a) intelligent
46. (a) ancestors
47. (b) accidents
48. (c) article
49. (b) Citizen's
50. (a) necessary

500 Commonly Misspelled Words

1. a lot–D*
2. absence–D
3. academic–D
4. accept–C
5. accident–C, D
6. accommodate–C
7. accumulate–C
8. accurate–C
9. accuse–C
10. ache–D
11. achieve–C
12. acknowledge–D
13. acquaintance–C
14. acquire–C
15. across–C
16. actually–C, D
17. address–C
18. adequate–C
19. admission–D
20. admit–C
21. advantage–C
22. advertise–D
23. again–D
24. against–D
25. aggressive–D
26. agree–D
27. alibi–D
28. all right–D
29. allow–D
30. almost–D
31. already–D
32. although–D
33. always–D
34. amateur–D
35. analysis–D
36. analyze–D
37. ancestor–D
38. annual–D
39. answer–C, D
40. anxious–D
41. apologize–C, D
42. apparent–C, D
43. approach–C, D
44. appropriate–C
45. argument–C
46. article–D
47. assistant–C, D
48. associate–C, D
49. athlete–D

50. attack–C
51. attempt–C, D
52. attendance–D
53. audience–D
54. author–D
55. autumn–D
56. available–D
57. average–D
58. awful–C
59. baggage–D
60. balance–D
61. balloon–D
62. barely–C
63. bargain–D
64. beautiful–C, D
65. because–D
66. beginning–C
67. believe–C
68. benefit–D
69. besides–D
70. between–D
71. bicycle–D
72. bookkeeper–C
73. bottom–D
74. boundary–D
75. bouquet–D
76. brief–C
77. build–D
78. bulletin–D
79. bureau–D
80. burglar–D
81. business–D
82. busy–D
83. calculator–D
84. calendar–D
85. calm–D
86. campaign–D
87. candidate–D
88. capital–D
89. career–C, D
90. careful–C
91. carriage–D
92. cashier–C
93. category–D
94. ceiling–C
95. cemetery–D
96. certain–D
97. character–D
98. chocolate–D

99. cigar–D
100. cigarette–D
101. circle–D
102. citizen–D
103. city–D
104. coincidence–D
105. college–C
106. comfortable–C
107. commit–C
108. commitment–C
109. committee–C
110. common–C, D
111. communicate–C
112. community–C
113. company–C
114. complete–C
115. completely–C
116. computer–C, D
117. conceit–C
118. conceive–C
119. conductor–D
120. conference–C
121. confidence–C, D
122. confusion–C, D
123. consequently–C
124. consider–C
125. convenient–D
126. convertible–D
127. cooperate–C
128. corporation–C, D
129. correspond–C
130. cough–D
131. counselor–D
132. country–D
133. courage–D
134. courteous–D
135. crisis–D
136. criticism–D
137. criticize–D
138. custody–D
139. customer–C, D
140. daily–C
141. damage–D
142. debt–D
143. deceive–C
144. decision–D
145. definite–D
146. definition–C
147. delicious–C, D

148. delight–C, D
149. democracy–D
150. dependent–C, D
151. descendant–D
152. desirable–C, D
153. desperate–D
154. develop–D
155. diamond–D
156. dictionary–D
157. different–C, D
158. difficult–C
159. dilemma–D
160. disagree–C
161. disappear–C
162. disappoint–C
163. discipline–D
164. dissatisfied–C
165. dissolve–C
166. dollar–D
167. ecstasy–D
168. education–D
169. efficient–D
170. eight–D
171. eighth–D
172. either–C
173. elevator–D
174. eligible–D
175. embarrass–D
176. employee–C
177. employer–C
178. enemy–D
179. engineer–D
180. enough–D
181. environment–D
182. equipment–D
183. escape–D
184. evident–D
185. exaggerate–D
186. excellent–C
187. except–C
188. excite–C
189. exercise–C, D
190. exhausted–D
191. exhibit–C
192. existence–D
193. experience–C, D
194. explanation–D
195. extraordinary–D
196. extremely–C

*These letters indicate the *All Spelled Out* book(s) in which the word appears.

197. familiar-*D*	249. improve-*C*	301. naturally-*C, D*	353. prediction-*D*
198. famous-*C*	250. incidentally-*C*	302. necessary-*C, D*	354. prefer-*C*
199. fantasy-*D*	251. independent-*C*	303. neighbor-*C*	355. preference-*D*
200. fascinate-*D*	252. indispensable-*D*	304. neither-*C*	356. prejudice-*C, D*
201. fashion-*D*	253. individual-*C, D*	305. nephew-*D*	357. prepare-*C*
202. fasten-*D*	254. inevitable-*C, D*	306. neutral-*D*	358. presence-*D*
203. fatigue-*D*	255. innocent-*C, D*	307. nickel-*D*	359. president-*D*
204. favorite-*D*	256. instance-*D*	308. niece-*C*	360. privacy-*D*
205. February-*D*	257. insurance-*D*	309. nineteen-*C*	361. private-*D*
206. financial-*D*	258. intelligent-*D*	310. ninety-*C*	362. privilege-*D*
207. flexible-*D*	259. interest-*D*	311. ninth-*C*	363. probably-*C, D*
208. foreign-*C, D*	260. interrupt-*D*	312. noticeable-*C*	364. procedure-*D*
209. frequently-*C*	261. irrelevant-*D*	313. nuclear-*D*	365. professor-*D*
210. fulfillment-*D*	262. jealous-*D*	314. nuisance-*D*	366. pronunciation-*D*
211. fundamentally-*C*	263. jewelry-*D*	315. obedience-*D*	367. proposal-*D*
212. furnace-*D*	264. judgment-*C*	316. occasion-*C*	368. psalm-*D*
213. further-*D*	265. knee-*D*	317. occasional-*D*	369. psychiatrist-*D*
214. future-*D*	266. knife-*D*	318. occur-*C*	370. psychological-*D*
215. gasoline-*D*	267. knob-*D*	319. occurrence-*C*	371. psychologist-*D*
216. gauge-*D*	268. knot-*D*	320. ocean-*D*	372. purchase-*D*
217. general-*D*	269. knowledge-*C, D*	321. odor-*D*	373. pursue-*D*
218. generous-*D*	270. laboratory-*D*	322. official-*D*	374. quantity-*D*
219. genuine-*D*	271. laundromat-*D*	323. omit-*D*	375. quarrel-*D*
220. gimmick-*D*	272. lavatory-*D*	324. opinion-*D*	376. radiator-*D*
221. government-*D*	273. legible-*D*	325. opportunity-*C, D*	377. receipt-*C, D*
222. governor-*D*	274. leisure-*C, D*	326. opposite-*C, D*	378. receive-*C*
223. gradually-*C, D*	275. length-*D*	327. optimistic-*D*	379. recipe-*D*
224. grammar-*D*	276. library-*D*	328. ordinary-*D*	380. recognize-*D*
225. grievous-*C, D*	277. license-*D*	329. original-*D*	381. recommend-*C*
226. grocery-*D*	278. liquor-*D*	330. outrageous-*C*	382. refer-*C*
227. guarantee-*D*	279. literature-*D*	331. pamphlet-*D*	383. reference-*D*
228. guidance-*C, D*	280. luxury-*D*	332. parallel-*D*	384. reliable-*C, D*
229. guitar-*D*	281. machine-*C, D*	333. pardon-*D*	385. relief-*C*
230. happen-*D*	282. machinery-*D*	334. particular-*D*	386. remember-*C*
231. headache-*C*	283. magazine-*D*	335. pastime-*C*	387. repetition-*C, D*
232. height-*C, D*	284. maintenance-*D*	336. peculiar-*D*	388. repetitive-*D*
233. heir-*D*	285. maneuver-*D*	337. perceive-*C*	389. represent-*C*
234. history-*D*	286. manufacture-*D*	338. performance-*D*	390. representative-*D*
235. holiday-*D*	287. marriage-*D*	339. permanent-*D*	391. respect-*C, D*
236. honor-*D*	288. measure-*D*	340. permission-*D*	392. responsibility-*C*
237. horrible-*D*	289. mechanic-*D*	341. philosophy-*D*	393. responsible-*C*
238. hospital-*D*	290. medicine-*D*	342. phobia-*D*	394. restaurant-*D*
239. humor-*D*	291. memory-*D*	343. physical-*D*	395. reversible-*C, D*
240. hundred-*D*	292. message-*D*	344. physician-*D*	396. rhyme-*D*
241. hygiene-*C*	293. miniature-*D*	345. pleasant-*D*	397. rhythm-*D*
242. hypocrisy-*D*	294. mischievous-*C, D*	346. plumber-*D*	398. ridiculous-*C*
243. hypocrite-*D*	295. misspell-*C*	347. poison-*D*	399. rival-*D*
244. ignorant-*D*	296. model-*D*	348. popular-*D*	400. roommate-*C*
245. immature-*C*	297. mortgage-*D*	349. possession-*D*	401. safety-*C*
246. immediate-*C*	298. mountain-*D*	350. possible-*D*	402. salad-*D*
247. immoral-*C*	299. muscle-*D*	351. practical-*D*	403. sandwich-*D*
248. important-*C*	300. mysterious-*C*	352. precious-*D*	404. satisfied-*C*

405. Saturday–D	429. specific–D	453. technique–D	477. useful–C
406. scene–D	430. spectator–D	454. technology–D	478. usually–C, D
407. schedule–D	431. sponsor–D	455. telephone–D	479. vacuum–D
408. school–D	432. standard–D	456. temperature–D	480. valley–D
409. science–D	433. stomach–D	457. tenant–D	481. valuable–C
410. scissors–D	434. straight–D	458. terrible–D	482. variety–C
411. secretary–D	435. strength–D	459. theory–D	483. vegetable–D
412. seize–C	436. strictly–C, D	460. tired–D	484. vehicle–D
413. seizure–C, D	437. stubborn–D	461. tobacco–D	485. vengeance–D
414. senator–D	438. studying–C	462. tomorrow–D	486. victory–D
415. sensible–C	439. submit–D	463. tongue–D	487. villain–D
416. separate–D	440. subtle–D	464. tragedy–D	488. visible–D
417. sergeant–D	441. sufficient–D	465. travel–D	489. visitor–D
418. shield–C	442. suggest–D	466. trial–C	490. volunteer–C, D
419. signature–D	443. suitable–D	467. trouble–D	491. wagon–D
420. significant–D	444. summary–D	468. truly–C, D	492. Wednesday–D
421. similar–D	445. superintendent–D	469. twelfth–D	493. weird–C
422. since–D	446. supervisor–D	470. uncommon–C	494. welcome–C
423. sincerely–D	447. suppose(d)–C, D	471. undoubtedly–C, D	495. welfare–C
424. society–C	448. surprise(d)–C, D	472. unfamiliar–C	496. wisdom–D
425. soldier–D	449. surround–C	473. unfortunately–C, D	497. wrap–D
426. solemn–D	450. survivor–C, D	474. unnatural–D	498. wring–D
427. source–D	451. susceptible–D	475. unnecessary–C	499. yield–C
428. souvenir–D	452. symbol–D	476. used to–D	500. young–D